SIX DEGREES of WAYNE KIMMEL

SEVENTYSIX CAPITAL

ACKNOWLEDGMENTS

Six Degrees of Wayne Kimmel grew out of the speeches I found myself giving across the country to packed rooms of students, entrepreneurs, and business people looking for a roadmap to success. First and foremost, I want to thank them for their interest; I continue to recognize myself in their wide-eyed aspirations.

This book wouldn't have come to be without a stellar team around me. Chad Stender is the greatest wing man any businessman can have, and a terrific networker and friend, as well. David Ongchoco was an immense help in getting my story down on paper, and the edits of bestselling author Larry Platt helped shape the narrative.

There are too many people in my business and private life to publicly thank, but let me call out just a few: My late partner Ian J. Berg, who taught me more than he ever knew; Tony Bifano and Scott Bohrer have been with me through all of this; and Jon Powell, my partner, with whom I connect both in business and personally.

There are countless family and friends who have shaped me; you know who you are, and how much I love you. I want to thank my investors for their support, all the interns and students who have inspired me through the years, the CEOs of my portfolio companies, and all my business colleagues and non-profit friends for teaching me so much. Both sets of parents — Morton & Marcia Kimmel, James & Nancy Schwartzman, and my siblings, Michelle, Karen and Larry.

Finally, a word to my wife Kimby and our kids, Sabrina and Hunter. You guys are who I do it all for and you continue to make me proud each and every day. I love you!

CONTENTS

Six Degrees
of Wayne Kimmel

You Never Score From The Sidelines

It was 7:30 in the morning and there I was, a 28-year-old nobody in a too-big suit, standing outside the Radnor Hotel in suburban Philadelphia, ready to accomplish my goal: To belong. To be where the action was. To be in the middle of everything. It was the late '90s, the apex of the Internet boom, and here's how I'd prepared: My right pants pocket was filled with my newly-printed business cards, "KimmelCorp." My spiel was that "I was funding and incubating startup Internet companies," though, truth be told, that was more hope than reality; I hadn't yet funded a single one. My left pocket was purposefully empty. Today's goal —as tomorrow's, not to mention the day after that—was to empty the full pocket of all my cards, while filling up the empty pocket with cards from those inside who I'd introduce myself to.

I was following the advice of a leading Philadelphia lawyer, Steve Goodman, a dealmaker I'd been introduced to by my father-in-law. "Meet everyone," Goodman, who would become an important mentor, had said. Go where the money is, he told me. Well, the money was having power breakfasts most mornings at Philadelphia's Conshohocken Marriott and the Radnor Hotel out on the storied Main Line.

Inside these restaurants were the guys who were changing the world. The guys I'd been reading about in BusinessWeek, Fortune and Forbes. I'd been obsessed by this thing called the Internet. I'd get the Silicon Alley Reporter and New York New Media Association newsletters and read about these tech meet-up events, and I'd just crash them. What was it Woody Allen once said? 80 percent of life is just showing up? Well, I'd just show up. Once there, I'd stare wide-eyed watching these Silicon Alley venture capitalists be the center of everybody's attention. The buzz around them was electric. Back home in Delaware, I was a law school graduate, working for my Dad at his success-ful Delaware law firm, struggling to pass the bar exam. Maybe that's because it wasn't my passion. I was too busy studying the Internet and the New Media world. "There's something happen-ing," I'd keep telling my Dad.

Inside the Radnor Hotel, there were the guys at the epi-center of what I just knew would be revolutionary change. At one table sat down-to-earth Walter "Buck" Buckley, CEO of In-ternet Capital Group, (ICG), the publicly-traded venture firm that, at the height of the dotcom boom, was valued at over $60 billion (now named Actua). At another table sat the courtly Bob Keith, cofounder of TL Ventures, at the time one of the largest venture capital funds in the Philadelphia region, which had been instrumental in bringing ICG and traffic.com, among many other companies, to market. Across the room, there was energetic Mark Walsh, then-CEO of Wall Street darling Verti-calNet and now the head of the Small Business Association's Office of Investments and Innovation. And there, in the middle of it all, at his usual spot, with a little brass nameplate on the table in front of him, sat Pete Musser, one of the Godfathers of Venture Capital, eating granola.

Musser was 70 by this time. I was well aware of his his-tory. He was 28 years old in 1955 when he had the idea to start a firm that would invest in young companies. He was the same age then that I was when, heeding Goodman's advice, I first started stalking him and the others at the Radnor Hotel. Musser's Safeguard Scientifics had played a major role in creating some of the world's most game-changing companies: Comcast in the '60s, Novell in the early '80s, QVC in the late '80s, and ICG and TL Ventures in the '90s. It's become trendy in recent years to talk about the "ecosystem" of companies that have all been nurtured together in Silicon Valley, but Musser created an ecosystem before anyone had ever applied the term to business. He was incubating startups at Safeguard long before the practice was part of the culture.

Musser's funds were mostly investing in Business-to-Business, or B2B, Internet companies. But I'd been seeing in New York that the next wave of companies to make it big were going to be customer-facing. So day after day, I'd show up at the Radnor Hotel, and night after night I'd show up at tech-related events, preaching my gospel. I didn't know anyone, though I had met Musser before. It was during a vacation to Nevis with my in-laws. A bunch of Philly vacationers got together for a New Year's Eve party. I found myself standing in the kitchen with this old guy who seemed very curious about my PalmPilot—remember those?

"What do you do with that thing?" He asked.

"I keep all my contacts in here, I put in notes about people that I get to know," I said.

"Let me see," he said. I explained that I'd learned from my Dad how technology could make your life more structured and convenient. In the pre-Internet '80s, my Dad's firm was one of the first to have a networked computer system that allowed him to attend all my basketball and baseball games without ever having to be out of touch with the office. Firsthand, I saw what a positive impact technology could have on our family life.

The guy seemed interested. "We should get together when we get back to Philly," he said.

"I don't live in Philly, I live in Delaware," I said.

"Well, same thing," he said. "Come up and see me. We'll talk."

Later that night, my father-in-law asked if I'd known who I was talking to; he told me that Pete Musser had been one of the founders of the Venture Capital industry. Pete who? Venture what?

Now, camping out at the Radnor Hotel, I started reminding Musser of our previous meeting. And, beyond Musser, I started collecting business cards. "Hi, I'm Wayne Kimmel, here's my card," I'd say to total strangers, holding it out and keeping my arm extended for theirs in return. Every day, the goal was to empty my right pocket and fill up my left. Once home, I'd email, call or even send a letter (remember this was the late '90s and not everyone had an email address on their business card) to everyone within a day of acquiring their card, looking to set up a breakfast, coffee or lunch, and then the cards I'd collected would go into a shoebox—thousands of them. There was no reason for these people to meet with me—I was a nobody. But I was heeding Steve Goodman's advice: I was meeting everyone. Because I was hellbent on belonging.

It's nearly twenty years and countless deals since those days when I was breathlessly pressing my card into strangers' hands every day, and when I think back on that overeager kid, I have to laugh. Because he didn't know what he didn't know. He had what we call in my faith chutzpah —he was not going to be denied. I think about that kid a lot these days, which is why I mentor so many ambitious young people. Because I know firsthand that, when you're young and hungry and dead set on making your mark, everyone tells you you have to "network."

THE GOSPEL ACCORDING TO WAYNE KIMMEL

Attending networking events, I fill up my
right pocket with business cards while leaving
my left pocket empty. My goal is to empty
my right pocket of my cards, while filling
up my left pocket with cards from those I'd
introduce myself to.

But no one tells you what that means. Or how to do it. And no one gives you anything. I learned at a young age to go get what you want.

This book uses my story to give you a game-plan. In these pages, you'll find practical tips, strategies and anecdotes that you can use to get ahead. Whether you're a young kid like I was, yearning to be in on the action, or someone already in the thick of things, the takeaway will be the same: It's all about building personal relationships. Here's what I learned when I was a hungry kid handing out my business card: No one will show up at your house and ask to help you. How do you meet the people that will become your most trusted and influential relationships? You have to go out and find them. You never know who they're going to be, so you have to cast as wide a net as possible by—as Steve Goodman counseled—meeting everyone. And then turning those contacts into relationships and opportunities. How do you do that?

By unconditionally helping others. That doesn't mean someone will automatically reciprocate and help you when you need it. But do it anyway. If you are in the business of building relationships, you can't worry about what your contacts will do for you. I believe that you should just keep doing things for them and eventually your time will come—they'll be there for you. That's when you know you have built a real relationship.

Mom and Dad taught my siblings and me when we were growing up that you should always help others. No matter how bad your day is, there is always someone who is having a worse one—and you can help them. You can lift them up by saying or doing something nice for them.

Why should you do this for someone you don't even know? Because we are all put on this earth to help each other and to make this world a better place.

I've now had the opportunity to invest in some world-class companies led by even better people. There was SeamlessWeb, which we sold to Aramark and is now public as GrubHub. There was Take Care Health Systems, which Walgreens made their in-store healthcare clinics. There was NutriSystem, the top performing stock in the country for five consecutive years. Some of my other companies were acquired by Intel, IBM, Yahoo! and Match.com.

My current investments include growing companies like Indiegogo, the largest global crowdfunding site, where Richard Branson is one of our co-investors; ReverbNation, a company that is changing the way that musicians are discovered and developed; CareCam Health Systems, which has developed a comprehensive health management solution; Dwolla, an online and mobile payment system; Whistle Sports, a global sports media company aimed at young people that includes, among our co-investors, NBC Sports, Peyton Manning, Derek Jeter and gold medal winning soccer player, Mia Hamm; StartUp Health, a company that is transforming healthcare that includes co-investors Mark Cuban, owner of the NBA's Dallas Mavericks, and AOL co-founder Steve Case and former Time Warner CEO Jerry Levin as Chairman, and Lindi Skin, a skincare company for people going through chemotherapy and radiation treatments, founded by Lindy Snider, the daughter of the late founder and owner of the Philadelphia Flyers, Ed Snider.

Even with all these deals, the power of personal relationships is still a lesson that keeps being driven home for me, nearly two decades after those mornings at the Radnor Hotel. Just recently, I was working to sell one of my portfolio companies to a large company. The company wanted to pay a lot less for my company than I wanted to sell it for. I was scheduled to meet with the CEO so I went to do my research on him to find a way to connect. I needed to find some common ground.

I searched the Internet. Unfortunately, he wasn't on LinkedIn. Nor Facebook. A Google search surfaced an article from his alma mater. Bingo! We both went to the University of Maryland. The article detailed that, like me, he was a huge sports fan. And there was a photo of him and his wife.

I went back to Facebook, searching for his wife's name. It didn't come up. But there was a woman with the same first name and different last name, who was from the city where his company was located, and who looked like the woman in the Maryland alumni magazine. I clicked on it and it was her—she used her maiden name on Facebook. There were photos of him and his family on vacation, and even ones of him coaching his son's basketball games.

When I went to meet him, there was tension in the air. He wanted to buy my portfolio company at a low price and I wanted to sell it at a high price. My guys from my portfolio company didn't think it was even worth talking about a sale. But if you're not in the game, you have no shot at winning. I opened the conversation with: "I hear you're a Terp!"

A big smile crossed his face. Our Terps were in the NCAA basketball tournament, and the first 15 minutes of our meeting was spent talking about our superstar freshman point guard, Melo Trimble. Then we bonded over coaching our son's basketball teams. By the time we got down to business, there was no distrust and we both wanted to make a deal. I didn't get all I wanted, but neither did he. We worked out a win-win deal, which would not have been possible if we didn't hit it off personally.

Stories like that one dominate my days, and are a testament to what I learned back when I was meeting everyone. Pat Croce, the great entrepreneur and former president of the Philadelphia 76ers, advised in his bestselling book that one of the secrets to success is the need to "stay in play." I learned that if you were in the room, you were in the game. That advice is always in my head. I needed to make sure that I was always present—shaking hands, smiling, being seen and heard. I studied the great networkers. I watched how they worked rooms. I observed how they were able to attend three or four events in the same night. I saw how they made people feel good when they spoke with them.

I hit the road and went to every event that I could get myself into. Honestly, I got into events that I wasn't "invited to." Guest list? What guest list? I'd hurry into the room, cell phone pressed to my ear, engaged in a loud, fake business conversation—"What do you mean he can't close that deal?"—in order to gain entry. (You'd be surprised how seldom you're stopped from going where you're not supposed to be if you just carry yourself like you belong there and dress the part). I went to every public forum, cocktail party and charity event where the heavy hitters would be. I made it my business to be in any situation or any place where top business leaders were getting together.

That was my job. I needed to get to know everybody. I was not expecting an invitation into their club, I was not expecting people to open their arms to welcome me...but I knew that I needed to be in the mix. I needed to be around the movers and shakers in the Philadelphia, New York City, Tel Aviv and Silicon Valley business communities. I made it my business to try to be everywhere. Because you never score from the sidelines.

How do you meet the people that will become your most trusted and influential relationships? You have to go out and find them. You never know who they're going to be, so you have to cast as wide a net as possible.

Every "No"
Is A "Not Yet"

It wasn't hard to make a few bucks in the mid '90s playing the stock market, so I had enough capital to invest in my first company. Despite the fact that my opening line was, "Hi, I'm Wayne Kimmel, I run KimmelCorp.com, and we fund and incubate startup Internet companies," I hadn't yet done so.

What I had done was rent an office in a smelly, old converted Bryn Mawr barn, because I wanted to be halfway between Safeguard in Wayne and our apartment in Philadelphia. My wife, Kimby, came to the office—once. "It kinda smells like a barn," she said. Welcome to the world of high finance, Kimmel-style.

Right before Christmas in 1998, I went to a tech event on the Penn State Great Valley campus. I did my usual spiel—"I fund and incubate startups"—but then something happened. A madman attacked me. This young, bespectacled guy, talking a mile a minute without regard for my personal space was in my face...and I was falling in love. The kid's name was Tony Bifano; little did I know that he'd go on to play a pivotal role in my life. He and his business partner had an idea for a website where students would come to get all their homework and, in the process, take part in a social community. There would be targeted advertising. I liked the idea of capturing a captive audience and using the Internet to provide them with a sense of community. (This was, what, six years before a Harvard undergrad in a hoodie started fooling around with a similar idea that would go on to change the world?) But most importantly, I liked Tony and his partner, Chris Mastergeorge (who would go on to become president of another one of my portfolio companies, Lindi Skin). Scratch that: Most importantly, Kimby liked Tony. "He seems like a really nice guy," she said, and thus was born my overriding investing philosophy.

From then on, I was committed to only investing in people who embody two characteristics: Smart and Nice. I know that sounds simplistic, and I know that it may seem counterintuitive when the cold, me-first calculations of Ayn Rand tend to dominate the bookshelves of the business elite. But I believe that, in the long run, success comes to those who help others and treat them with respect. I learned this from watching my Dad build a great law practice while staying true to Golden Rule values. And I learned it growing up in Delaware with the famous Biden family. Beau, who would go on to become the state's Attorney General only to die far too young of brain cancer in 2015, was one of my good friends. What I learned watching him and his father, Joe, was the power of putting others first. As important as these men were, they always had time for everyone else–without regard for what was in the relationship for them in return. Call it karma or just the law of averages, but the more they gave, the more they got. Go ahead and celebrate Steve Jobs' coldness or Elon Musk's aloofness. Many successful people treated others nicely on their way to the top. And when they did, it meant that people were rooting for their success. I saw that in Delaware.

So being nice was always part of my investment calculus. I knew fast-talking Tony was smart—he was so smart, sometimes it was hard to keep up with his train of thought—but Kimby confirmed for me that he was nice, and that sealed the deal. Besides, Tony was a kindred spirit in terms of his boundless energy. People had long been telling me I was crazy when it came to my aspirations, and yet that never slowed me down. It's not about what people say or think. Like me, I could tell that Tony was all about moving forward and thinking positively. To me, every "no" had always been a "not yet." Tony's force-of-nature presence told me he was the same way. Here's a guy with the force of will, I remember thinking.

Tony's company was egenda.net—the first I'd invest in. I helped get Tony and Chris an office underneath a nail salon in Bala Cynwyd. The fumes of those chemicals would waft downward as we strategized over cold pizza and beer. They were thrilled, though, because before the nail salon office they'd been in a cramped house in Manayunk—one step up from a garage, with wires hanging out of windows in order to secure dial-up Internet access.

For the first time, I opened that ol' shoebox and put my network to work for one of my companies. I'd bring some important guys in suits to what we called the nail salon office, including Steve Goodman, David Reibstein, the well-known Wharton marketing professor, and Howard Ross, then with Arthur Andersen and now a partner in the billion dollar LLR Partners private equity firm. I helped them raise $5 million, and then we merged egenda.net with College Directory Publishing in Conshohocken, PA. They were a ten-year-old company that printed yellow page phone books for colleges across the country. The company had about 100 employees and high-strung Tony became the CEO of this much larger company. The plan was to take the company public, but then the dotcom bubble burst.

Still, we did okay. More important, it was a tremendous learning experience. I learned that I could activate my network. But I also learned that I didn't have as much money as I'd thought. I had enough to make an investment in Tony and Chris, but I was going to be hard-pressed to invest in more companies. And, when you're raising money from your network, they want to hear that you have some skin in the game, too.

So in the summer of 1999, I started to figure it out. There are these guys who raise venture capital funds to invest in companies—how does that work? As usual, I asked Steve Goodman. "The guy you need to talk to about that is Pete Musser," he said.

So there I was, on the Safeguard campus for an afternoon meeting with Pete. I was on the second floor of the 800 building, the center of activity on an eight building suburban office campus. My adrenaline was pumping. I was like a kid at Disney World for the first time.

I had actually practiced my spiel beforehand. "Mr. Musser," I began, "I'm here because I want to tell you I want to start a venture capital fund."

He looked up from his desk. "Stop right there," he said. "You can't do that."

Now, Pete was a down-to-earth, soft-spoken man. So this stopped me in my tracks. I wasn't looking for his permission; I was there to tell him what I planned to do and to get some advice.

"I can't?" I asked.

"No," he said. "Here's what you're going to do. Yes, you'll start a venture capital fund. But it will be based here at Safeguard. You'll make it synergistic with our other funds and it'll be a seed fund. Your successful deals will flow into our PA Early Stage Fund. Your fund will be a $10 million fund. If you can raise $9 million, I'll invest $1 million."

There was a pause. For one of the few times in my life, I was speechless.

Musser looked at me, as if to say, What are you waiting for? "Get out of here and go do it," he said.

I jumped up, shook his hand, and floated down the stairs of the building. A legend of venture capital had just told me I'm going to be on his campus and my fund would be part of the Safeguard family, and all that entails. I'd spent two years banging on doors and now...now, I'd been invited in.

And *all* I needed to do to belong was raise $9 million. In the car, I called my Dad, and breathlessly recounted the meeting.

There was a pause. "Well," he said, sounding cautious. "Congratulations, I guess. I don't understand any of this. You better get on the phone with that lawyer friend of yours."

He was right. Steve Goodman had to be my next call. I didn't know what the next step needed to be, but I suspected it had everything to do with the art I'd spent the last two years trying to master: Networking.

How do you turn contacts into relationships? By unconditionally helping others. If you are in the business of building relationships, just keep doing things for others and eventually your time will come.

When You're Small, Act Big

I didn't know it at the time—heck, what I didn't know at the time could fill its own book—but when I set out to raise my first fund, what I was really doing was amassing my air cover. What do I mean by that? Think of it in terms of going into battle. If you're in the army, you need the air force to have your back so you can take that hill. Well, I needed help taking my first hill.

So, just as Dad instructed, my first call was to Steve Goodman to tell him about the challenge laid down by Pete Musser and to basically ask him...okay, now what? What's that line from the old Talking Heads song? "Watch out — you might get what you're after." Now I'd gotten what I was after — an invitation into the club by none other than Pete Musser. But that raised an even more daunting question: What the heck do I do once I gain entry?

"First, of all, are you kidding me?" Steve said when I breathlessly recounted to him my conversation with Musser. "This is unbelievable. How did you do this?" To Steve, I was just some fast-talking kid. How'd I get Musser on my side?

"I don't know!" I said, as surprised as he was. "But now I need to know. What do I do now?"

Steve told me to settle down and not worry about anything. "I'll handle everything," he said. "There are legal documents we have to execute, which I'll get in order. But first, I want you to meet someone. His name is Ian Berg, and he has been a friend and client of mine for thirty years."

Ian J. Berg was 59, thirty years older than me. He'd just retired after selling the financial services firm he found, Copelco, to Citigroup. Ian had founded Copelco in 1972 and, thanks to his leadership, it had grown to more than $5 billion in assets and $500 million in revenue, with 1,600 employees. As a result of the sale, he had a non-compete in the financial world—with the exception of venture capital. He lived in Cherry Hill, New Jersey, and had been spending most of his time with his five grandchildren. "My wife and I just bought a place in New York and I'm spending a lot of my time in the City," he said when I reached him on the phone. "Let's meet there."

It just so happened I was planning on being in New York for a new media conference—and even if I didn't have such plans, I would have told him that I did. "Let's have breakfast at the Plaza," I said.

In Judaism, we have a yiddish word beschert—which means "meant to be." It's a beautiful, romantic word: Kimby and I, for instance, are beschert. But not long into our initial breakfast, it became clear to both of us that Ian and I were beschert, as well. Ian had been chairman of the Philadelphia chapter of the Young Presidents Organization. YPO is a global network of young chief executives with about 22,000 members in 125 countries. Talk about networking; YPO members bonded with and helped one another on multiple levels. Ian was particularly passionate about YPO. He'd go away on ski trips with the younger YPO members, and always return invigorated. It wasn't long before we were playing Jewish geography and it became apparent that he was in the same YPO group as Kimby's uncle, and that he was quite socially friendly with Kimby's aunt and uncle.

"We've met before!" Ian exclaimed. "I remember stopping by your in-law's place at the shore and dropping something off for Kimby's grandmother!"

I only had a vague recollection, but no matter. We were connecting. We had a great conversation, in which I told him about all the cool things happening in the tech and new media space; I told him I had to head back to Philly and would he want my pass for that day's conference? It could give him a taste of the world I was talking about. He jumped at it and called me later, impressed. "I think you're right," he said. "There's something going on."

Over the next ten days, we talked multiple times a day, feeding off each other's enthusiasm. Soon, we were finishing each other's sentences. Finally I said, "Look, Ian, we seem to get along. Let's be partners."

"Listen, kid," he said. "I've got five grandkids. I travel a lot. I've got YPO. I don't have time to start a new business. But if you take care of all the details, I can show you how to do this. We'll do some good things together."

We put up an equal amount of capital to get our first fund started. My pitch was he knew the dads, and I knew the sons. In that way, our reach was greater together than it ever could be on our own. But Ian had one caveat that some might have seen as a deal breaker: he wouldn't raise any money. "Remember," he kept telling me. "I'm never asking anyone for money. I don't fundraise. You fundraise. You get the money and I'll show you how to invest it and how to structure these things."

So, if I raised all the money, he'd be my 50/50 partner. There were those who said that wasn't a great deal for me. After all, I was going to be doing way more than fifty percent of the work for fifty percent of the windfall. But had I taken that position, that would have just been my ego talking.

Remember, I needed air cover. Ian was my air cover, as was Pete Musser and Safeguard Scientifics. If you're going to invite me in, I'm setting up shop. At Safeguard, they first gave me space in a closet — literally. It was in the Eastern Technology Council building, and all the women who worked in that office liked to joke that when I came out of my "office": "Look! Wayne is coming out of the closet!" I laughed as heartily as anyone.

Soon, I upgraded to another small office, albeit one where co-workers hadn't previously been hanging their coats. It was a heady time on the Safeguard campus. Limos were all over the grounds, dropping off and picking up Masters of the Universe. Walking by Pete Musser's office one day, I saw him huddled with none other than Dan Quayle, who was seeking Musser's advice about what to do with his life after the vice-presidency.

I was a wide-eyed kid on the campus, but I also used my access to my advantage. That campus was every bit as much mine as it was Pete's. I became known for giving tours of the campus. I'd walk a prospective investor or entrepreneur into the offices of Safeguard's main building on the campus, and also visit SCP Partners, Safeguard International, PA Early Stage, TL Ventures, EnerTech Capital and usually wrap up my tour in ICG's brand new office, with its screen on the wall showing its stock price ticking up every day —worth more than General Motors at one point.

And I'd point out the quirkiness of the place, too —like one of ICG's managing directors, who would do nothing but walk around campus all day with his Blackberry to his ear. "Who's that?" I'd be asked after a guest would see him for the third or fourth time, walking and talking, walking and talking.

"Oh, that guy," I'd say. "He's one of the ICG guys. He just walks and does conference calls all day. Watch, he'll come back around in about twenty minutes."

THE GOSPEL ACCORDING TO WAYNE KIMMEL

The myth is that the top tech companies Google, Facebook and LinkedIn were created by tech geniuses sitting around in their pajamas writing code in their bedrooms or in a garage. The dirty secret is that the success of these companies really came from collaboration, making contacts and developing relationships.

Being able to say I was on the Safeguard campus and that Ian Berg was my business partner meant that I was real. When I got in front of a mover and shaker, I wasn't just some 29-year-old lone wolf kid. I was someone who had the backing of Pete Musser and Ian Berg. I couldn't ask for a better protective halo. When I was in a room with an investor, I needed that. The fact that Musser and Berg believed in me gave me all the credibility in the world.

You can't just go out cold and expect to be successful at fundraising. I needed the endorsement of guys like Musser and Berg, but I also had to do a ton of pre-work before getting in to pitch potential investors. I needed to be known—I needed a potential investor to have heard about me before he sat down across a table from me. You want other people talking about you — that's always preferable to talking about yourself. So I needed the halo effect of publicity. But, remember, this was 1999. There was no such thing as social media. So I had to work with the existing traditional media.

I befriended reporters and columnists at the Philadelphia Daily News, Philadelphia Business Journal, and Philadelphia Inquirer, among others. These guys were churning out business profile pieces every day; they didn't have time to be running all around town searching for new leads. But I could. I started feeding them stories — and not just about me. I'd give them tips about stories in the tech community. That way, when I did give them something about me, I'd already helped them out on other fronts.

I'd scour their writings for the names of potential investors to approach. If I saw that a mover/shaker was being honored with an award at a charity gala, I'd write a check to the cause and show up and introduce myself.

I also took a page from my Dad's playbook—literally. Back in the '80s, he was one of the first I'd seen to take an old-fashioned yellow sticky note pad and have his own law firm printed on it, along with "To" and "From" lines, with space below for a handwritten note. When he came across a newspaper clipping about someone he knew or about some stranger he was impressed by, he'd tear the page out, affix a sticky note from Mort Kimmel with a note of congratulations and send it along. I started going through countless sticky note pads.

Every week, the Philadelphia Inquirer would report on the comings and goings on local Boards. I'd send off notes. If I'd read that a local bold-faced name had been appointed to a prominent board, a note from me followed: "Congratulations!" I'd write. I don't think most people take the time to do this type of thing, but it was the best way I knew to stay front and center in the minds of those that could be helpful to my portfolio companies or my venture capital fund.

The myth today in my industry is that Google, Facebook and LinkedIn were created by tech geniuses sitting around in their underwear writing code in their bedrooms or in a garage with a couple of friends. The dirty secret is that the success of these companies really is more about everything I'm talking about: Collaboration, working rooms, making contacts, building relationships. Mark Zuckerberg and the other tech icons of today were once feeling their way just like I was, finding investors, loyal customers and press contacts. They may have coded in their underwear, but, trust me, they were out and about pressing the flesh—and they were fully dressed.

It's all about hard work—even the actual act of asking for money. Today, my portfolio company StartUp Health, is at the cutting edge in terms of training healthcare startup companies how to pitch. The team talks about how you need a 59 second pitch and you have to think very carefully about your words and messaging. They actually have CEOs stand in front of a mirror with a stopwatch and practice their riff. Sometimes, they'll bring fifty companies onto a stage and each will get 59 seconds to make a presentation and critique the hell out of them.

Now, I can't say my investment pitch was that finely cali-brated back then. I'm sure I wasn't ever at 59 seconds. But even then I sensed the degree to which the fundraising pitch is a mix of art and craft. People have so much going on in their lives, you have to realize you're not the center of their universe and you've got to leave them with something memorable.

So you have to figure out what that something is. And it's not a litany of facts: The minimum investment amount, the profit participation, the management fee, or even your business plan. It's none of those things. It's about leaving whoever you're pitching something they're never going to forget about you. It's the personal connection. In that sense, it's really all about the pre-work, the research. You need to Google every person you are going to meet with and also search for them and their com-pany on Facebook, LinkedIn, Twitter, Instagram, etc. and try to find some common ground.

You may find that someone grew up in the Bronx like my Dad—that's a connection. You may find that someone is a sports fan and has season's tickets to the Eagles—that's a con-nection. You may find that you both worked for the same com-pany at some point in your career—that's a connection. Then when you are meeting with that person you can bring up these common nuggets.

In addition, I have learned from some of the great busi-ness people that I have been fortunate to be exposed to that it's not always what you say, but the questions that you ask. Listening is key. So when making a pitch, it's as important to ask questions and then sit back and listen and learn about their story. What made them successful? What makes them tick? What are they most passionate about? Then, once you get this kind of information and knowledge about them, you can tailor your pitch accordingly and truly connect with them. Starting with my very first venture capital fund, one of the things I've always left with prospective investors is a sense of no-holds-

THE GOSPEL ACCORDING TO WAYNE KIMMEL

Investors have so much going on in their lives, you have to realize you're not the center of their universe and you've got to leave them with something memorable.

barred frankness about the risks of investing in the venture capital industry and startup companies. "Do not invest with me if you can't lose all the money you're investing," I tell them. "I'm in the high risk business. This is not a mutual fund or even a hedge fund or a stock you can sell tomorrow. A venture capital fund is a ten-year deal. You're giving me your money and you're betting that I'm going to make you multiples of your money. With each company I invest in, I'm either going to hit a homerun or strike out really badly. If I go 3 for 10, you're going to make a ton of money. Just like in baseball— you're a Hall of Famer if you go 3 for 10. Don't forget that I'm telling you this and don't invest with me if you can't flush all this money down the toilet."

Sophisticated investors would get it. This is my play money, they'd tell me. This idea of identifying, investing in, and helping passionate entrepreneurs build game-changing businesses is fun, they'd say. Others would say they were too conservative, that they didn't like writing a check for $1 million dollars without the guarantee of a return. That told me venture capital wasn't for them—which I'd say to them. Back when I started, according to the National Venture Capital Association, there were maybe 200 VC firms in the country. Today, it's still a small industry—less than 500 firms. Venture investing is very time intensive, and you better want to work with wild and crazy people who have some pretty out-there ideas. It's not for everyone.

But if you're intrigued about it, as most are when I can get in front of them, it's the coolest thing in the world. I tell investors we're swinging for big returns and when you make 20 or 60 times your money — which I've delivered—you're changing other people's lives by seeing to it that their dreams come true. How cool is that? I'm like an entrepreneurial A&R guy, the music industry talent scout who is out in the clubs finding the next big hit. (And I know from one of my companies, ReverbNation, a top music industry artist management site, that the A&R guys are still out there, in search of what's next). So instead of you doing one-offs as an individual, or angel investor, with entrepreneurs coming to you every week asking for money, let me handle it for you. I have the team and infrastructure in place to handle this deal flow. And, while we're at it, I'll say, keep in mind that the stuff I invest in is pretty exciting. I provide some pretty good stories for you to share at cocktail parties. Invest with me and you can casually bring up in conversation that you're an owner of Indiegogo, the world's largest crowdfunding company. Or if a buddy of yours uses his phone to order from Grubhub, you can say, "Hey, I was an early investor in that" because we were the only venture fund in the world to back that company when it was SeamlessWeb.

Of course, I didn't know all this at 29. Back then, my pitch was about being plugged in to this world the investor knew little about, and convincing them that I had the vision and contacts to discover young companies that would change the world. That's where the halo effect helped immensely. And each investor after that only added further to the halo.

A particularly big moment came when Brian Tierney and I sat down for breakfast at—where else?—the Radnor Hotel. Brian had just sold his advertising and public relations firm, Tierney Communications, and he was on top of the world. He'd long been one of Philadelphia's leading movers and shakers, and I'd read about him for years. A part of me couldn't believe I was sitting here, eating an omelette with *the* Brian Tierney. And we weren't just talking; we were hitting it off. It quickly became apparent that, on the surface, we seemed very different. Brian was raised super Catholic and I'm Jewish. He's a Republican and I'm a Democrat. And yet, from the first moments of our breakfast, a budding bromance was brewing. I could just tell that he was a good guy. Like me, he was passionate about life and business and committed to making things happen.

Now, I have no formal training in public relations, but I think Brian was impressed that we both spoke the same language when it came to using the press to help benefit our respective causes. We bonded over how to cultivate relationships with newspaper writers, over messaging, over branding. At that breakfast, Brian told me something I've never forgotten: "People don't hear you the first time you tell them something, or the second time, or the third time, or the fourth time. Maybe it registers the fifth time. Don't be shy about repeating your message." That's something I've taken with me through the years. Today, I tell all our CEOs that, if you tweet something at 9am and someone's in a meeting and doesn't check his or her twitter feed until the end of the day, they're never going to see your post. Don't be afraid to post it again at noon or 5pm. "When you think you've done too much social media, do more," I tell our CEOs. What's the worst that will happen? Someone might unfollow you? Big deal.

Why is this important? Because in the startup world, you're small but you have to act big—perception is reality. So how do you act big but not look like you're just acting? By thinking carefully about the message you send out about who and what you are — and by sending it often. I learned that in 1999 from Brian Tierney, whose investment in me then was yet another addition to my halo effect.

Brian and I have gone on to do great things together, including being co-investors in NutriSystem. He also is on the Board of Directors of NutriSystem and has provided the management team with tremendous marketing and public relations advice. When Brian bought The Philadelphia Inquirer in 2006, he asked if I wanted in. Are you kidding? What a huge challenge! And a great opportunity to work with him and the group of investors and team members that he assembled.

Just as at Safeguard, once I was on the Board of the newspaper, I started giving tours of the storied newsroom. But unlike at Safeguard, where energy was in the air and you felt like you were in the middle of something great happening, the Inquirer newsroom felt like a library. How can it be so quiet here? I'd wonder. Why aren't there TV screens displayed, blaring up-to-the-minute news? Why is there no energy in the air? The trend exemplified by Silicon Valley startups like Facebook and Google, with people collaborating closely together, had taken the country by storm...except here. Though it was a fascinating learning experience, I knew our stewardship of the newspaper was going to falter when I'd walk through that newsroom and see that the workplace was still arranged with each reporter and editor literally in their own silo'd cubicle.

But back in 1999, all I knew was that, thanks to the help of Musser, Ian Berg and Brian Tierney, I was starting to build some momentum. I learned by doing, and I learned that you never knew when networking opportunities might present themselves. Kimby was pregnant and we had recently moved to the Philadelphia suburbs from Center City. One morning, I was out walking my brother's dog when a woman walked up. She was putting fliers on all the neighboring houses.

"Hi, my name is Connie Williams, I'm your State Representative," she said. She handed me one of her fliers. I might have grunted something, put the flier in my back pocket, and wandered off. My head was elsewhere—no doubt thinking about my fund and just how was I going to raise all that money?

When I got back to the house, I pulled the leaflet out of my back pocket. I instantly felt bad that I hadn't talked to this woman. Even then, I believed that you could do well and be nice at the same time—and here I didn't really live up to the values my parents had modeled for me. I wasn't mean, mind you, but I wasn't nice to her. I didn't stop to have a moment of real connection. This woman was working so hard, knocking on all those doors, and she merely wanted to talk with me. The least I could have done was have a conversation with her.

I started to read her literature. If you needed to change your voter registration, I learned, she could do that for you. Well, I needed to do that, since we'd just moved. So I wrote her an email, apologizing for not stopping and talking with her, and asking her to help me change my voter registration. I guess I was feeling guilty about my rude behavior, because I also asked if she would have breakfast with me.

She very quickly responded and accepted my offer. At breakfast, she was very nice. She asked about my family, and I gave her chapter and verse on Kimby's pregnancy. When I told her I was raising a venture capital fund, she started peppering me with questions. But they weren't questions any random curious person would ask. She asked about my philosophy, my thesis and about the terms of the fund: the minimum investment amount, the management fee, the carry percentage, etc. These were sophisticated investor questions.

I didn't think much about it until the end of our breakfast when she asked me to send her my investment documents. I did so, even though I had my doubts. Would a local politician be able to risk a significant sum of money in a venture capital fund?

About ten days later, I received her executed investment documents with a large check attached.

Turns out, Connie's maiden name was Hess—as in Hess Oil. Her father, Leon Hess, owned the New York Jets. To this day, Connie is a friend and supporter. I had no idea. How telling is that? What if I'd been so wrapped up in myself that day I was walking the dog that I never thought twice about that hardworking politician who wanted a few moments of my time? I'd have deprived myself of a friendship and a smart investor. It may sound trite, but my whole life is proof that it's true: One of the greatest keys to being great in business is to just be nice to everyone. It doesn't matter who they are. Because there is always a chance that you will stumble upon your most valuable contacts in the least expected of places.

THE GOSPEL ACCORDING TO WAYNE KIMMEL

Brian Tierney told me something I've never forgotten: "People don't hear you the first time you tell them something. Maybe it registers the fifth time. Don't be shy about repeating your message."

You Just Have To Be There

Raising my first fund is when I perfected my own personal art of networking. I wanted to be on every mover and shaker's radar screen, and the only way to do that is by working hard and being present. Networking is fairly simple; what's hard is actually doing it.

It starts with the very basic act of showing up. You have to get off the couch. You have to go out. You just have to be there. You have to be present. You have to go out and meet people. It is the way for your build up your contacts. You have to go to events. You have to try out new things. You have to expose yourself to new ideas and people. Emailing, social networking and connecting online is nice and helpful, but it is not enough.

To win the lottery, you at least have to purchase a ticket. You have to be out there. You need to meet the people who can help you achieve success. After you meet them, you need to build a relationship with them.

Again, this can get exhausting at times, but it's extremely rewarding if you do it. There will be nights when you would rather hangout with your family or friends instead of going to a networking, political or charity event. You need to just get up and go. You need to summon that inner strength and go.

Many times you will not be rewarded immediately for your networking efforts. Go anyway. This is a long game. Building relationships through networking is like a marathon, not a sprint.

Networking is time consuming and people ask me the question all the time, "How do you have all the time for all this?" I don't. I make the time. Because the people who are willing to invest their time to really build their network are the ones who get the big deals done. The people who do the little things that nobody else does, like following up and sending thank you emails, are the ones that end up sealing the big deals.

Look, if networking and getting deals done were easy, everyone would be doing it. Everyone would be succeeding. The next time you go to a networking event, if you look carefully, you will be able to spot those who are working to make it happen. You will see the people who are on a mission.

You'll see people standing around eating and drinking, not really taking advantage of the opportunity to meet as many people as possible in the room. And you'll see people who are only talking to their friends and colleagues. And then you'd see someone like me. Someone lurking outside a bathroom waiting for some mover and shaker to emerge from it so I can say hello, exchange cards, and try and leave him with something to remember me by.

I have had many friends and business colleagues who would go with me to these networking events, but most of them eventually didn't have the stamina or drive to keep going. They wouldn't do the breakfast meetings anymore. They'd say things like, "I have to get home to see my kids" or "My wife needs me home" or "I'm too tired." I understand all of that stuff. I know what it's like to be tired and to want to spend time with family. But I don't use them as excuses. Instead, I figure out a way to do it all. It helps that Kimby understands that this is the job.

We've even stopped off at events on our way to vacation down at the Jersey Shore. Kimby, our kids and the dog would wait in the car while I'd run inside for twenty minutes, just enough to make sure my face was seen before heading back out to the car. Kimby understands that today is an investment for the future…even if today is a vacation day.

It does get exhausting, pulling yourself out of bed to attend a 7:30 am breakfast networking event, attending a networking meeting at lunch, giving speeches in the afternoon, and going to events after the work day is over. And then there are those weekend conferences after a long week of work.

Not only is it exhausting, it's often uncomfortable. You walk into a room, alone, grab a drink, look for a familiar face. Nowadays, when I see somebody standing alone, I go up to them and talk to them because I was once the guy standing there alone going, "Who should I talk to?..Should I just leave?…This is ridiculous, there's no one important in this room. I'm just leaving. It's a waste of my time to be here."

And the next thing you know, of course, something happens. You strike up a conversation. You get a business card. You make a connection. You don't know where it will lead, but you're suddenly full of possibility.

One of my favorite movies is "Wedding Crashers." The characters played by Vince Vaughn and Owen Wilson are on a mission to meet women and their strategy is to crash weddings. Like me, they do their research and find out where a "good" wedding is being held. They find out the dress code and just show up and walk in. They just show up. No need for an invitation. They do their thing. In one scene, one of them says, "We're brothers from New Hampshire. We're venture capitalists." I knew I loved these guys.

Like those guys, when I was raising my first fund, I figured out where the important people were going and I showed up, whether it was at Conshohocken Marriott, The Radnor Hotel,

The Four Seasons or the Rittenhouse Hotel. I remember, as part of my due diligence, I read about the history of the power breakfast on the website of New York's storied Loews Regency Hotel:

> On any given weekday morning—from 7 AM to 10 AM—a collection of shiny black town cars are lined up three-deep outside Loews Regency Hotel. Inside, the tables are filled with movers and shakers from the worlds of Wall Street, entertainment, media and politics. As they discuss business and close deals, they are simultaneously observing a morning ritual that has been ongoing for close to 40 years—the Loews Regency New York Hotel's "Power Breakfast."
>
> The tradition began informally in the mid-70s during New York City's financial crisis when Bob Tisch—founder of Loews Regency New York Hotel—invited the city's business and political leaders to his Park Avenue hotel for breakfast before the workday started. They spent the time discussing ways to help the city recover from bankruptcy. Recognizing the significance of its participants, Mr. Tisch dubbed the meetings "Power Breakfasts" and in doing so, forever changed how business was done in New York.
>
> Today, the Power Breakfast stands as one of the most iconic dining experiences in Manhattan, offering local New Yorkers and hotel guests the perfect opportunity for people watching—and the chance to dine among some of the most powerful professionals in New York City. Only Loews Regency New York Hotel starts the day with the iconic Power Breakfast—and you're invited.

Once I figured out where to go, I'd show up, usually dressed in business casual attire. I'd wear nice jeans, a nice shirt, and a sport coat. I rarely wear a tie even when I wear a suit. And I'd make sure to have that pocketful of business cards ready to distribute—because they are just as important as anything I am wearing.

Being armed with business cards in my right pocket makes me feel comfortable in a networking situation. They're the best icebreaker. You really do not have to have a creative opening line if you have a business card. All you need to say to someone that you walk up to is, "Hi, my name is _____, here's my business card."

Then say, "Can I please have your card?" And after that just say, "Thank you." Of course, if you now are feeling more comfortable after that exchange, you can look at the business card that you just received from the other person and ask them questions based on it, like "I see you company's name is _____, what kind of business are you in? Or, "What is your role at _____ company? How many years have you worked there?"

Networking got a lot easier for me when I thought about it like this...my only goal was to empty my right pocket and fill up my left pocket. All I needed to do was to give out cards and ask for cards. It's so much easier than my single days when I was trying to ask a girl out. That's far more complicated!

Sometimes at one of these breakfast places if someone looked important, I'd try to give my card to them and strike up a conversation and get shot down. "I'm not sure who you think I am," I have been told by a number of people, "but I'm just here on vacation with my family to have breakfast." I learned to brush that off, and then try again with someone else. You can't get too up or too down when you are out there networking.

Sometimes people I'd give my card to would ask who I was meeting for breakfast. This was a slight problem because the whole point of what I was doing there was to meet people so I could have a breakfast meeting there some day in the future. I needed to be quick on my feet and make up a name of a person and then change the conversation to another topic. This networking thing truly is an art.

Yes, I was ambushing people before they'd have their first cup of coffee of the day. Damn right. I knew I was starting to

I tell all the CEOs and execs at all of my companies that, if you tweet or post something on social media at 9 am and someone's in a meeting and doesn't check their twitter feed until the end of the day, they're never going to see your post. Don't be afraid to post it again at noon or five o'clock or before you go to bed.

get somewhere when people started recognizing me and I really knew I was on to something when CEOs would enter the lobby, see me, and say "Morning, Wayne."

The more breakfasts and networking events I went to, the more I learned, the more people I met and the more comfortable I became doing it. And I developed strategies on how to do it more successfully. Take the name tag, for example. I love name tags. They allow you to walk around and, without saying anything, promote yourself. The name tag lets others know who you are—which is precisely why you go to these events in the first place.

Believe it or not, there's actually a name tag strategy. You should always wear your name tag on the right side of your shirt or jacket. Most people will clip it on the left side of their jacket because there's a pocket there for a handkerchief or pin it in the hole on the left lapel of a coat because there is a hole there. But that's for a flower! It is not meant for a name tag.

See, when you shake another person's hand with your right hand, his or her eyes will see your name tag while making eye contact with you. If the name tag is on the left side, your acquaintance has to look across your body while shaking your hand. Your goal is to make a connection...so why make it harder to connect?

Or take the name tag table. I learned early on to watch people closely as they approach it and to make a mental note of which tags they pick up. I'd have done enough due diligence that I'd come with a list of names of people I'd want to meet. Well, if I paid close enough attention, I could meet them all at the registration table. I could say hello to them while we're putting our name tags on and then walk with them into the event.

I've even loitered around the name tag table and Googled names that I'd see there, or looked them up on Facebook on LinkedIn, in search of information I can use when having a conversation. What college did he attend? Does she have kids?

Everyone wants to tell their story. You've just got to give them a chance.

I also try to make friends with the organizers of an event and the people that are working behind the registration desk. Many times they will give you the inside scoop on what is going on, who will be attending and if there is a special guest that could be helpful to you.

I also learned early on how important it is to have a Wingman. Most people feel awkward rolling solo. Back then, I'd often have my man Tony Bifano by my side; today, it's Chad Stender, my Director of Operations at SeventySix Capital, who is along for the ride. Still, I never minded networking alone. In fact, I learned how inanimate objects could substitute for the live wingman.

The bar can be your Wingman. Waiting in line for a drink, your target has nowhere to go. Start talking to them and you'll get five to ten minutes of uninterrupted time. Same thing with the buffet line. They are your captive audience as you load up on the roast beef. But it's important to realize you're not there to eat—even if you're in the buffet line. Once, I went to a networking brunch with the CEO of one of my companies. We got in the buffet line and we started talking to people as we loaded our plates. I got to the end of the buffet and put my food down.

"What are you doing?" My Wingman asked.

"We came here to meet people," I said, putting down my plate and getting back in line.

Other ways to connect with people at events? Walking to and from the bathroom offers the chance to get some quality time, as does washing your hands in the bathroom. (But I draw the line at the urinal. That's where the conversation ends).

At any gathering, there is usually someone else who is also there by himself. I'd introduce myself. Chances are he was feeling as uneasy as I was and—presto!—we'd both have instant Wingmen.

I also learned to gravitate toward a room's focal point, usually a piece of art or a large buffet or a fountain. People tend to move toward items like these, providing opportunities to strike up conversations. You also don't get self-conscious because you're standing in a corner by yourself.

I learned to take my time in these rooms. You do not need to rush into a networking event. Enter the room slowly. No need to be nervous. Survey the room. Look for any potential familiar faces. Look to see where the food is located. See if there are any important people there that you recognize. Again, the more you practice this the better you will get.

If you see a friend or acquaintance, walk up to them and say hello. It's a great way to get warmed up and get yourself ready to meet people that you do not know. Do not spend the whole time with your friend. This kind of warm introduction allows you to sort of ease your way into your networking mode.

The most successful networkers are okay getting out of their comfort zone. Once again, use your friends to warm up and eventually you can use them as a crutch to allow you to meet people they know or people that are standing close to them. Remember, you are there to hand out your business card and collect other people's cards. You already have your friends' contact information and you can hang out with that person later. Go work the room!

If I don't see anyone that I know, I may make the decision to walk towards either the bar or the food, whichever one has more people around it. This allows me to think about my next networking move. It also allows me to further determine who is in the room. It gives me a different angle to look around more and to see who else is there.

I like to pull people into my conversations and introduce them to one another. It's a nice thing to do, but it also shows you're in control of the room. It's a power move. A lot of politicians and big business people use it. They'll introduce you to somebody else and it allows them to either stay in the conversation or go talk to other people.

Another move that I like to do is to ask someone that you are talking to if there is someone in the room that they would like to meet. It is a way to help someone right then and there.

Basically, networking is about connecting and finding common ground with others. No one told me how to do this. But I had the pressure of having to raise $9 million hanging over my head—so I had to figure it out. There were some crazy moments. Like that time someone at an event complimented my tie. "Thank you," I said.

"My daughter's Bat Mitzvah is in a few weeks," he said. "That tie is a perfect match with my daughter's dress." What did I do? I took that tie off and gave it to him right then and there. Why not?

These little things add up, and so it was in 1999 and into 2000. We had started fundraising in the fall of 1999 and we ended in March of 2000. The challenge had been to raise $9 million and I walked in with $19 million!

So in March of 2000, I walked into Pete Musser's office and announced, "I'm here for my million dollar check."

"What do you mean?" Pete asked.

"You said that if I raised $9 million, you were in for $1 million, and I have some great news, I actually raised $19 million," I said.

He paused, smiled, got up from behind his desk and called to his assistant to cut me a check. And just about when he was going to pat me on the back he stopped. He shot me a puzzled look and said, "Wait a minute, why am I writing you a check for the full $1 million? How much is the first capital call?"

Huh? I had no idea what a capital call was. I must have looked confused.

"That's how funds work," Musser said. "You don't take all the money at once and put it in the bank, you take a percentage of the money and then you call the rest when you need to make investments."

"No, that's not how we're doing it," I said, pretending that not holding a capital call was a purposeful decision.

Pete gave me his check. And then I called Ian.

"Why didn't we set this up as a capital call fund?" I asked Ian.

"Because I didn't want to have to deal with all the administrative BS of calling people when we need the money," he said. "This way, we have the money, it's in the bank whenever we need it."

It was the smartest decision we ever made. That month, March of 2000, the NASDAQ hit an all-time high. A couple of weeks later, disaster struck. The bubble burst. Webvan, Pets.com, Lycos, Kozmo.com …everything was crashing. People thought it was all over. The Internet was over. I was worried, too. But I knew that markets go up and down, and it's a pretty good time to build companies in down markets.

And no one would be building companies for a while, because so few had any cash left after the crash. But guess who had $20 million in the bank?

There will be nights when you would rather hangout with your family or friends instead of going to a networking, political or charity event. Go anyway. You never know who you will meet. This is a long game. Building relationships through networking is like a marathon, not a sprint.

There's Got
To Be A
Better Way

My buddy Steve was on the phone. Today, Steve Krein is the CEO and co-founder of StartUp Health, one of my portfolio companies. But Steve was also my alter ego back in the day at the University of Maryland. I remember sitting on the roof of our fraternity house, trying to convince Steve to go with me to law school in Delaware. He did for our first two years of law school and then he went to New York and discovered this thing called the Internet. He provided the first clue that something was happening out there in "Cyberspace." Without Steve, I may have never gone down the VC road.

We've remained close all these years. In fact, my sister, Karen and I helped set up Steve's brother, Howard, the Chief Medical Officer of StartUp Health and a surgeon at Thomas Jefferson Hospital in Philadelphia, with Ashley Biden, the vice president's daughter. They eventually married. We may live in a big world, but our lives really take place in small villages.

And that's why Steve was calling on that day in 2000, when I was trying to decide what to do with all this cash Ian and I suddenly had in the bank.

"Wayne, you're going to get a phone call from Jason Finger," he said.

"Jason? I remember Jason," I said. Jason had been one of my fraternity brothers at Maryland and was Steve's roommate in the frat house.

"Yeah, well, Jason and his friend from law school—"

"Jason went to law school? I didn't know that," I said.

"Yeah, he went to NYU," Steve said. "His friend's name is Paul Appelbaum. They're both at two major law firms in Manhattan. They've got an entrepreneurial idea. They want to enable people to order food online. I gave them your information and they're going to reach out."

That's how SeamlessWeb—which I would eventually help sell to Aramark and is now publicly traded on the New York Stock Exchange as GrubHub—first came to my attention. Because of my network of relationships.

Jason and Paul's idea grew out of the same thought process that has given birth to disruption throughout our history: Whenever and wherever progress is made, you can usually trace it back to someone saying to him or herself, "There's got to be a better way."

Jason and Paul were young lawyers at big New York law firms, the type of firms that work their ambitious associates to death. They were in the office every night till midnight—or later. At around 8 pm, they'd order dinner. And that's when the trouble started. They could purchase up to $50 per dinner per night and were expected to charge that amount to whatever client whose account they were working on at the time.

They didn't have corporate cards. They'd have to use their own personal credit cards to pay for the food delivery and hang on to the receipt. Then they were expected to fill out an expense form, attach the receipt, and hand it to their respective assistants, who would then turn the paperwork over to accounting. The reality of this system soon hit: Come month's end, Jason, Paul and so many of their friends had drawers full of random receipts piling up in their desks. It was the end of the month, which meant they needed to pay their credit card bills, but reimbursement from accounting would invariably take too long to come through.

They thought: There's got to be a better way. What if there was a system where young lawyers could go online, order their food, put in their client code, and include a tip. The restaurant would receive the order and send the delivery out. And the law firm's accounting office would have an instantaneous record of who was charging what. That was key: In many cases, lawyers like Jason and Paul were closing multi-hundred million dollar deals. Typically, such deals closed with a flurry of late night, round the clock sessions, with food strewn all over conference tables. A deal would close and then, a month later, accounting would advise that a few thousand dollars of food costs from those last, harried nights had not been figured into the deal. The lawyers were in a quandary: They'd just sent their client a final invoice for fees of, say, $500,000 and now comes this straggler of a bill for a couple of thousand more dollars for food? Most firms just ate that expense, if you'll pardon the pun.

Maybe it was because of my legal background, but once I saw Jason and Paul's business plan for a web-based solution to this mess, I got that they were on to something. They had a solution to a real world problem. But as a VC, it's never too early to think about your exit. Let's say this works, I thought. Who's going to buy it? How am I going to pay back my investors?

So, yes, I was attracted to this idea—they were calling it SeamlessWeb—because I saw the need and I saw that it was solving a business problem for law firms. But even then I knew my gut wasn't enough. I've always believed in finding experts and listening to them. That takes humility, and discipline. You have to acknowledge that there are people who know more than you, and then you have to seek them out and be open to what they say—even if it conflicts with what your gut is saying.

Going over Jason and Paul's business plan before I even met them, I had a thought: Aramark should buy this company. Aramark was a Philadelphia-based food services Fortune 500 corporation. I'd become friendly with Richard Wyckoff, the president of Aramark's refreshments division. We'd been introduced by mutual friends. He was active in YPO and we'd played golf together. I decided to invite him to my first meeting with Jason and Paul.

Now, you might think that's premature. After all, I hadn't even met with these guys yet, and here I was bringing along an outsider to help me size them up. But I wanted to know if this was going to be worth my time. I wanted to know what an expert thought.

So we had a meeting, and after Jason and Paul made their case and left, I turned to Richard.

"What do you think?"

He let out a low whistle. "If they can do what they say they can do," he said. "Aramark should buy this company."

Now I had my game plan. I'd help SeamlessWeb get off the ground, and I'd keep Richard and Aramark appraised of the progress along the way. One of the things I learned over the next few years as we laid the groundwork for such an exit was that, even though Aramark ran cafeterias for law firms and businesses, providing the opportunity for office workers to seamlessly order in food helped Aramark's bottom line. How? They'd no longer have to invest in all that overhead to keep their cafeterias open into the night. Gone would be the days that the lights stayed on and the staff stood at the ready just to serve one guy a hamburger at 8 pm. This way, Aramark could shut down its cafeterias after lunch and still capture some revenue from food delivered in after hours.

SeamlessWeb was an instant hit. Sure, it involved having to install computers at some restaurants—not every business was online back in the day—but it was embraced by companies and restaurants alike. We went from law firms to investment banks and hedge fund firms, and the restaurants loved it because SeamlessWeb paid them in a timely manner. They didn't have to send bills; at the end of the month, the account was settled. After 9/11, many of the companies who were forced to relocate from lower Manhattan no longer had cafeterias in their new digs. The need for SeamlessWeb was even greater. By year five, with hundreds of thousands of customers using the service in New York City, then we opened it up to consumers.

We were the only venture capital investor in Seamless-Web. We invested more than $1 million of our first fund into the company. Aramark bought it in 2006, and we made close to thirty times our money on the deal. This one investment alone more than paid back that first $20 million. Of course, Seam-lessWeb would become GrubHub, which today has a multi-billion dollar market cap and is traded publicly on the New York Stock Exchange. For us, it was a homerun right out of the gate, and it wouldn't have happened without nearly flawless execution by the management team and two key relationships: The call and referral from Steve Krein and the expert advice from Richard Wyckoff, which was followed by years of staying in touch with him and keeping the possibility of an eventual sale front and center in his mind.

At the same time, another company we invested in was taking off. NutriSystem had been founded in 1971 by Harold Katz, who would go on to own my beloved Philadelphia 76ers basketball team and win the NBA title in 1983 with Dr. J and the late Moses Malone. But after Katz sold the company it had gone through a succession of owners and fallen on hard times.

We received a unique opportunity to join a Philly-based investor group that included Mike Hagan, George Jankovic and Pete Musser to invest in NutriSystem in 2001. We invested and Ian joined the NutriSystem board. His resume and reputation gave it a lot of credibility.

Hagan and Jankovic ran the company as well as I had ever seen – thoughtfully, smartly, and incredibly strategic. An opportune moment occurred that helped propel the company forward when Hagan met Dan Marino, the Hall of Fame Quarterback from the NFL's Miami Dolphins, on a golf course on Kiawah Island, South Carolina. They connected immediately and soon thereafter Marino became NutriSystem's pitchman. NutriSystem focused on growing its male consumer base by airing commercials of Marino explaining his 22 pound weight loss on male dominated networks like ESPN and CNBC. I was there for Hagan and Jankovic, making strategic introductions and suggestions during our great run together. NutriSystem's stock price climbed from 60 cents a share to over $75 and Hagan was named Forbes CEO of the Year and graced the cover of the magazine.

By the mid-2000s, the cloudy skies that hovered over all of us during the dotcom bust were clearing. Our fund was doing well and others were coming back. And the best was still yet to come.

THE GOSPEL ACCORDING TO WAYNE KIMMEL

I love name tags. They allow you to walk around and, without saying anything, promote yourself. The name tag lets others know who you are—which is precisely why you go to networking events in the first place.

At an event, I survey all the name tags on the table and if I see a name of person or the name of an interesting company I want to meet, I will google them and sometimes look them up on Facebook or LinkedIn, in search of information I can use to start a conversation with them.

How I Became "The Maitre'd"

My friends tease me about my constant networking. One buddy says that I'm separated from every entrepreneur around the world by no more than six degrees, like I'm the startup version of Kevin Bacon. I'll go with my brother, friends and my son to an Eagles game or quite frankly, any sporting event, and I'll make it a point to walk the concourse, shake hands, and make small talk about the game with whoever I see that I recognize.

I get some good-natured ribbing about it, but what needs to be understood is that that is how deals happen. Think about what you've heard from me so far; how many opportunities have come about simply because someone who I'd taken the time to get to know thought to run an idea past me?

Case in point: In 2004, I got a call from Linda Holliday. Linda was the President and co-founder of something called the Medical Broadcasting Company, which had a studio and offices on Rittenhouse Square in Philadelphia. It operated under the radar—few knew about MBC—but it was a visionary business for its time. Basically, they started doing video for the pharma industry and had transitioned to become the industry's premier digital agency.

Linda saw things before other people did. She and I weren't in any deals together, but I'd love to sneak away with her to Tequila's, a great Philadelphia Mexican restaurant, for long lunches during which I relentlessly picked her formidable brain. Her clients included all the big healthcare and pharmaceutical companies, many of which were located in the outlying Philadelphia suburbs, and Johnson & Johnson. She was a thought leader in terms of what the future held for major companies from a communications standpoint. She was pushing her clients toward having a dynamic digital presence. Some scratched their heads and wondered, "Why would Tylenol need a website?" Or "Why does Viagra need to be online?" The answer was that Linda saw that the future of corporate communications in consumer-facing industries would be much more interactive and immediate. The days of sending information out into the atmosphere on your schedule were not only quickly becoming a thing of the past, the commercials and infomercials on which she'd cut her teeth were increasingly viewed as self-serving.

Linda and I would talk often about the future, but it wasn't like I ever had an agenda. And that's what I love about my business. We had these really great conversations, often over spicy burritos, and they were energizing because they were full of ideas—but we were also laying the groundwork for helping one another whenever and wherever the need would arise. We never knew where a conversation might lead. Which is why you have to be open to everything and always stay in the mix.

Such was the object lesson that day in 2004 when Linda called. "You've really got to meet a friend of mine," she said. "He wants to do something, but he's not sure what."

Her friend was also her longtime client, Peter Miller. He was the President of Janssen Pharmaceuticals, a division of Johnson & Johnson. He was also the guy who brought Splenda to market for J&J's division McNeil —those little yellow sugar substitute packets. To this day, at breakfast meetings, I like to pick up one of those packets and point out what few know: that it's distributed by McNeil in tiny Fort Washington, PA, just outside Philly, and tell people about Peter's involvement with the product.

Anyway, if Linda thought Peter was someone I should know, it was done. We agreed to meet at the Capital Grille in Center City, Philadelphia; he said he'd be bringing his business partner, Hal Rosenbluth. As a precursor to our meeting, Peter sent me a "business plan" he and Hal had put together. The night before, I reviewed it...and I couldn't stop laughing. In fact, I still have it framed today, in my home office.

It wasn't a business plan so much as a testament to the greatness and successes of Peter and Hal. It began:

> Introducing Hal F. Rosenbluth and Peter Miller. It's not all that common that the sun, the moon, and the stars come into alignment. For Hal Rosenbluth and Peter Miller, it all happened during the summer of 2004. Hal Rosenbluth had recently completed the sale of his multi-billion dollar global travel management company, Rosenbluth Travel, to American Express, and Peter Miller, after successfully running several of Johnson & Johnson's larger companies, had decided it was time to take advantage of this experience and leverage it against new business opportunities...Eventually a moment comes in business, a moment of truth, a moment of fleeting opportunity, a moment of change that forever can alter the way a business is conducted. Hal and Peter have built careers on recognizing that such a moment is upon them. They are visionaries who can see things in a business that other can or will not.

The rest of the plan contained quotes from others, attesting to how visionary Hal and Peter were. I must have read that plan five times before our meeting, thinking I'd missed something. Like: What's the business? But, nope, this was it. The whole plan. Linda wasn't kidding: They wanted to do something together but they didn't know what. All they had was their bios —but great bios they were, which is why I was intrigued.

The day of our meeting, I got to the restaurant first. Peter walked in and he looked as I expected: hair perfectly parted, pressed khakis, a nicely-tailored buttoned-down shirt. But this other guy? What a trip. Hal Rosenbluth sauntered into the restaurant wearing cowboy boots, worn jeans, and a T-shirt. He slumped back in his chair while Peter filled me in on his own background.

Finally, I turned to engage Hal. "And I read a couple of things about you, Hal," I said. "I know you built and sold a multibillion dollar travel business to American Express. And I saw that the Wall Street Journal called you the 'City-Slicker CEO,' and that you have a ranch somewhere?"

"Yeah, that's me," he said, still slouching down.

I tried another tack. "So I read the stuff you guys sent me," I said. "Let me ask you, what do you want to do? How can I help you?"

"Well, you're the startup guy, right?" Peter said.

"Yeah," I said. "I invest in startups."

Hal leaned forward. "So can you help us?"

Huh? "Well, help you do what? What do you want to do?"

"We think we can do something disruptive, something incredible," Hal said. "Something to change the world."

Okayyyy. Rather than press for specifics, I did what I do: I sought a more personal connection. The conversation turned to sports; these were guy's guys, and I liked them instantly. They definitely passed my "smart and nice" test. We talked about Hal's ranch and his love for the outdoors. He mentioned that, in addition to Linda's referral, the late Fred Blume, then the head of the powerhouse law firm Blank Rome and one of Hal's closest advisors, had told him he'd better sit down with me because Fred used to refer to me as the "startup guy."

That was heady stuff to hear. Remember, I was all of 33 at the time. SeamlessWeb was on its way and NutriSystem was starting to take off, but I hadn't done near as much as either of these two guys. I'd never known executives like these two. They both had built billion-dollar consumer-facing companies—and they were asking *me* to help *them*.

"We've done a lot of things," Peter said, "but we've never done a startup. Would you be willing to hang out with us and show us that world?"

So what did I do? I started meeting them for breakfast at the Conshy Marriott. I started introducing them to the CEOs of the companies in our portfolio. In New York, they visited the offices of SeamlessWeb and met CEO Jason Finger. That was an eye-opener for them. "This startup world is crazy," Hal said upon his return. Remember, both Hal and Peter were used to a very corporate structure. That's not the case in the startup world. Not only doesn't the CEO have an assistant arranging his daily schedule, he takes out the trash. For Hal and Peter, it was a culture shock.

This went on for months. Breakfasts, meetings, phone calls: Still, there was no idea, other than to do something game-changing and disruptive. The closest we got was some musings that they wanted to do something in the healthcare space. That led me to bring Hal to breakfast with NutriSystem CEO Mike Hagan as part of our mutual learning tour. I'd been soaking up knowledge from Hal these many months; he was, true to his look, a gunslinger. I don't think he ever had an unexpressed thought.

I nearly choked on my omelette when, as Mike was telling us about his rapidly growing business, Hal blurted out: "So how much do you want for the business?"

Mike, who is not nearly as in-your-face as Hal, was taken aback. He explained that NutriSystem—which was public, after all—wasn't for sale. But Hal persisted. "No, seriously," he said. "I'm putting together something disruptive in healthcare and

The bar itself can be your Wingman. Waiting in line for a drink, your target has nowhere to go. Start talking to him and you'll get five to ten minutes of uninterrupted time. Same thing with the buffet line. He or she is your captive audience as you load up on the roast beef.

I'm thinking of having a weight loss piece to it. So how much do you want?"

The meeting ended uncomfortably, with Mike shooting me a look as if to say, "Wayne, what's with this guy?"

But that was Hal. I loved how bold he was. Finally, a couple of months later, early in 2005, I got a call from Hal. He had it. The idea I'd waited over six months for was ready to be revealed.

"We figured it out," he said. "We're going to open health-care clinics inside of pharmacies, staffed by nurse practitioners, to take care of people's common ailments."

"You mean, like, inside drug stores like CVS, RiteAid and Walgreen's?" I asked.

"Exactly," Hal said. "You're going to walk into your pharmacy and get checked out by a nurse practitioner, which is almost a doctor. Let me tell you about nurse practitioners. The first two years of their training is the same as the first two years of medical school. You basically learn enough those first two years to be a primary care doctor, because the next two years are when the emphasis is on specialization. So you come in and get seen by a nurse practitioner and then you get your prescription filled right there—"

"Hold on," I interrupted. "Can nurse practitioners prescribe medicine?"

"You bet. No one knows that," Hal said. "It's going to be called 'Convenient Healthcare.'"

Talk about two words that rarely go together: Convenient and healthcare. I thought: This might just be crazy enough to invest in.

Remember how I vetted SeamlessWeb with my friend from Aramark? I returned to that playbook here. I'd recently joined the board of Einstein Healthcare Network and gotten friend-ly with our CEO Barry Freedman. I asked what he thought of Hal and Peter's plan. "That could take business away from the Emergency Room, which is actually a good thing," he said.

Wait —how could losing customers be a good thing?

"Because when people come to the Emergency Room, it costs us and the health insurance companies a lot of money and time," he explained. "We only want real trauma cases in the ER. We need to start training patients that when you have a common cold or back strain, you go to your doctor. But a lot of doctor offices open late and close early, so it's inconvenient."

My next step was a family doctor I knew, who thought it was a terrible idea. I actually brought him to meet with Hal and Peter—I wanted them to hear the case against their idea. "You're going to take business away from family physicians," he told them. "And nurses can't diagnose as well as we can. We're doctors."

Okay, so there might have been a little male chauvinism behind that reaction. But other doctors I spoke to seemed similarly threatened by the idea of losing patients to these clinics. But the more I thought about it, I was able to work up a compelling response: "Are you open at 7pm? Do you open at 7am?" The answer, of course, was always, "No, they have to either come in the next day or go to the Emergency Room."

Precisely. A lot of people I talked to thought the idea was doomed. I heard a whole lot of what ifs: What if someone has a heart attack at the clinic? What if the liability is too high? What if a nurse practitioner overprescribes a medication? What if there's a misdiagnosis?

You know what? "What if" can be a prescription for paralysis. It's good to be cautious and to think through every angle, but I believed deep in my gut in Hal and Peter could do it. These were guys who were going to do something big. Hal's philosophy appealed to me. "The goal in business is to discover an unknown, unmet need, fulfill it, and then run as fast as possible," he'd say. A lot of companies look for the road less traveled; Hal likes to go where there is no road...and build one.

Still, before committing, I embarked on one more act of due diligence.

At that point, a company called MinuteClinic was already doing a version of what Hal and Peter wanted to do. Later, they'd be our main competition; at the time, MinuteClinic had rolled out inside Target stores. There was one in Maryland. Well, I needed to be a clinic customer. One afternoon I hopped in my car and decided to go undercover.

On the way, I started to worry. I wasn't sick but I'd have to pretend to be. But Kimby is super superstitious. I could hear her voice in my head, warning me not to invite sickness upon me by lying about it. A couple of hours later, I was at Target, where I had to search to find the clinic. Once there, I filled out a form and was quickly called into a room for a consultation with a nurse practitioner. I told her I'd recently flown and my ear was still clogged. A white lie, right? She checked me out and said she couldn't find anything. "I wouldn't prescribe you anything," she said. "But here are some over the counter products you can use." Soon, I was on my way back. Wow, I thought, that was so easy. I was in and out in twenty minutes, with very little in the way of paperwork.

Once I got home, I called Hal. "I'm in," I said. I pledged $1 million, roughly what we invested in SeamlessWeb and NutriSystem. Soon, Hal reached his target of a $12 million raise. But then came another head-scratcher. "I'm not starting the company yet," he said.

Huh? Turns out, he wasn't taking money from investors until he'd secured his first contract with a pharmacy. Within a couple of months, he'd gotten deals with RiteAid and other chains. Soon, our Take Care Health was up and running and Hal created something called The Convenient Care Association. As other competitors started popping up, Hal brilliantly realized there needed to be a credible trade organization that established the best practices for such a new industry. He hired a Chief Nurse Practitioner—not a Chief Medical Officer—to run it, and the Association partnered with the Nurse Practitioner Association of America. The CCA started holding conferences around the country and drafting industry guidelines. So who do you think was seen as the Founding Father of the Convenient Care movement? Hal Rosenbluth, naturally! And it made our company, Take Care Health Systems, the industry leader.

Just before Thanksgiving in 2006, Hal called and summoned Ian and me over to his office right away. That wasn't out of the ordinary. When Hal Rosenbluth has a pressing matter, there's usually not a lot of time spent waiting to deal with it. This certainly was a pressing matter.

At this point, Take Care had opened about 15 to 20 clinics. Things were promising, but still touch and go in terms of longterm viability. Now Hal had some news.

"Here's the deal," he said. "Walgreens wants to work with us exclusively. They're massive. We'd roll out in their stores across the country. But to do the deal, they say I've got to have $50 million in the bank by the end of the year. Or the deal is off the table."

Gulp. It was already Thanksgiving, for crying out loud. Getting money people to do a deal between Thanksgiving and Christmas is virtually impossible. "Well, Hal, you've got great relationships with Goldman Sachs and other banks, right?" Ian said.

"They don't want to do this," Hal said.

There was silence. He knew we didn't have $50 million. But he also knew that we had a different type of capital: the power of relationships. I looked at Ian. "What about Bill Lautman?" I asked.

"If anyone can do it, Bill can," Ian said.

"Who is Bill Lautman?" Hal asked.

"He's probably the only healthcare investment banker crazy enough to take on this assignment with enough connections to get it done in time," Ian said.

The clock was ticking. Ian's daughter was friends with Bill, a workaholic independent healthcare banker with an entrepreneurial streak. He'd love the challenge. We got him on the phone and he came down from New York the next day. In less than seven weeks, he didn't pull together just $50 million...Bill raised $77 million.

Now, once Walgreen's and Take Care Health started going down the road of a partnership, it became clear to all involved that it just made more sense for Walgreen's to buy us. And that's what happened. For several hundred million dollars.

That would not have happened if we hadn't introduced Hal to Bill Lautman. Walgreen's probably would have concluded these jokers aren't real and Take Care never would have gotten acquired.

Once again, it was contacts and relationships to the rescue. That's why Hal gave me my nickname. Hal gives everyone a nickname; oftentimes, they're quite politically incorrect. Mine was "Maitre'd." I didn't get it at first, but then Hal explained it. "Wayne, you know everyone and it's your job to help other people—just like a Maitre'd."

And Bill Lautman's nickname? Well, the guy pulled something off no one else could have. Batman, of course.

SeamlessWeb, NutriSystem, Take Care Health Systems. These were all investments from my first fund, $20 million that returned over $68 million. We were one of the top performing venture capital funds in the United States. Not bad for a first time out, huh?

By 2007, we were ready to start raising capital for another fund. It was barely eight years since I hovered outside the Radnor Hotel restaurant every morning, hoping to give away a stack of business cards, trying to get noticed by the likes of Pete Musser. Now I was in the game and riding high. Little did I know that some dark clouds were forming ahead.

Startups are not for the faint of heart. These aren't corporate deals. They are intimate relationships. You're going to be with this person through boyfriends and girlfriends, weddings, childbirth, divorces, graduations, family celebrations and tragedies.

If You Don't Take A Shot, You'll Never Make A Basket

Meet me in Cherry Hill," Ian said. "There's something I need to tell you."

This was out of character for my partner. I drove over to his house in Cherry Hill, New Jersey, with a sense of foreboding. Something was up.

It was mid-2007 and we were planning on raising $50 million for our second fund. We'd already gotten commitments totaling $23 million. I couldn't wait; after the success of our first fund, I felt some pressure—we had to show we weren't one-hit wonders. But mostly I felt excited. I couldn't wait to get back out there, because, as rare as it is to come across the likes of Mike Hagan, Jason Finger and Hal Rosenbluth, I'd been meeting some great young entrepreneurs who I thought we could help become successful.

That's when Ian told me he had cancer. And not just any cancer: Pancreatic cancer. I raced home and Googled it and didn't like what I read. It's particularly lethal. I was shattered. My friend and mentor was gearing up for the biggest fight of his life and I pledged to myself and to him that I'd be there for him every step of the way.

As for the business, Ian wanted to stay involved. He had been true to our original delineation of duties and hadn't fund-raised. As a result, I told him I felt comfortable sending a letter to all our investors—my contacts—telling them the news of his illness and offering a refund, if they so desired. No one asked for their money back.

A word about Ian as a partner. By now you know I'm led by my enthusiasms—which is a quality I look for in our CEOs. Too many people in this world start with the word, "No." I'm attracted to those who begin at "yes" because I'm a "yes" kind of guy. And Ian was a great check on me. "Wait, hold on," he'd say. "Are you sure? Have we really done the due diligence on this? Have you really gotten to know who this person is?"

He was the best cross-examiner I'd ever met—and he didn't even have a law degree. When we'd sit down with a CEO for one of those feeling-out meetings, Ian could be in-your-face and intimidating, but also inspirational. He'd ask the CEO to define success. Invariably, he or she would start talking about how much money they'd made. That's when Ian would strike. "Why are you sitting here asking me for money if you were so successful?" he'd ask. "Why do you need other people's money? You define success as selling a company for a million dollars? Let me explain something to you. We're venture capitalists. We're here to make a minimum of ten times our investment in your company. Which means you have to build a really big company. We're trying to hit homeruns. My partner here, Wayne, he's going to do anything and everything for you. He's got contacts you won't believe. I've got experience you won't believe. But we have to be on the same page. If you think success is building a million dollar company, we're not right for each other. If you want to build a billion dollar company, we're your guys."

Sometimes, when Ian was making a CEO feel like a sixth-grader, I couldn't help but smile or laugh, and he'd kick me under the table. "You are not to show any emotion," he'd tell me later. "I'm trying to find out how these people react."

If a CEO barked back at him, he'd love it. This was sport to Ian, and he loved when he came across a kindred fighting spirit. He enjoyed making people uncomfortable. He'd ask, "How do those numbers go to the moon like that? I don't understand," and then, like any good prosecutor, he'd find five other ways to ask the same question—because sometimes, on the fifth or sixth question, you get a different answer. "This isn't our money, Wayne," he'd tell me. "We have an obligation to our investors. Sometimes people are just really good actors."

It was because of Ian that I first started to develop my theory of investing in people who were smart and nice. Ian thought ahead. He knew that companies don't get built overnight. NutriSystem and SeamlessWeb both took nearly eight years. The idea that companies go from startup to IPO in a convenient and tidy transition is fiction. I learned from Ian that you're going to spend real time over many years with the people you invest in—and you better be sure they're the type of people with whom you want to have a longterm relationship. These aren't cold, corporate deals. These are intimate relationships. You're going to be with this person through boyfriends and girlfriends, childbirth, divorces, family tragedies. And that's just on the personal side. On the business front, startups are full of stress. Ian knew that our job was to simulate stressful situations in a conference room meeting with CEOs we may want to invest in. Because if they can't handle being challenged in a conversation like that, how will they handle the rejection that awaits in the startup world? Because one thing is certain: You're going to be rejected. You will get rejected by customers, by venture capitalists, by other entrepreneurs, and by friends who will tell you you're crazy.

That's only natural. If you're doing something that is truly revolutionary, that is truly game-changing, then you're doing

I like to pull people into my conversations and introduce them to the person I am talking to - It's a nice thing to do, but it also shows you're in control of the room. It's a power move.

something others can't fathom yet. You're inventing the future. That's what Albert Einstein was getting at when he reportedly said, "If at first the idea is not absurd, then there is no hope for it." If you're pursuing something new, people are going to think you're nuts—until, in retrospect, they conclude that you were a genius all along.

Ian taught me that our job was to be a type of detective, looking for clues in the psychological makeup of men and women that could tell us whether they had the true drive, passion and resiliency to take on the stress of being a visionary – a real entrepreneur.

There were some dark days in 2008, as Ian battled his illness and the economy tanked. There was a lot of fear — fear for Ian's future, fear for the future of the American economy. But we also knew that in bad economic times the winners in the long run are those who are willing to innovate. Our job was to double down on innovation.

We closed the fund with the $23 million we'd raised and went to work. Ian battled his cancer valiantly for 18 months before succumbing to the disease. At his Shiva, his sons told me how they always knew when their Dad was working on one of our deals. He'd sit at the kitchen table with the legal documents spread before him while eating chocolate ice cream. That's another thing I learned from Ian: No one cares about the legal documents until there's a problem—and then it's all about the documents. So he'd go over a deal's documents as close as any lawyer I've ever seen. I had to laugh at this image of Ian, his face buried in deal documents while shoveling ice cream into his mouth, because for years we'd all have a good laugh about how any documents that went home with him to Cherry Hill always came back smeared with chocolate stains.

To date, portfolio companies from my second fund have been bought by IBM, Yahoo! and Match.com. When my portfolio company Omek Interactive was acquired by Intel, it made me one-for-one for successful investments in Israel. Companies like Adwerx, CareCam Health Systems, Dwolla, Indiegogo, StartUp Health, ReverbNation and Whistle Sports are all maturing every day. When I look at my portfolio, I like to say that these companies are lottery tickets representing some potentially big time winnings. We have others like Lindi Skin and Thrive Commerce that could make it big too.

For some time, one of those lottery tickets was Fisker Automotive. But Fisker didn't actually work out as planned. When you swing for the fences, you're going to strike out a bunch, too. Fisker is one of those near misses that gets across just how thin the line is between success and failure.

In 2008, I got a call from Hunter Biden, Joe's son. Hunter told me about Henrik Fisker, the legendary designer of the Astor Martin car. Fisker was starting his own electric car company and was going to be in Delaware to meet with the newly elected Governor, the businessman Jack Markell. The plan was to build the cars in the old GM plant in my home state of Delaware, and I instantly wanted to be a part of it and a part of Markell's plans to reinvigorate the Delaware economy. Just as a previous generation had made Delaware a banking and corporate incorporation capital, now the thought was to lure innovative businesses to the state.

I brought Tony Bifano with me to the Green Room at the Hotel Du Pont in Wilmington, Delaware for dinner with the Fisker team. And they laid out the plan for Tony and me, two non-car guys. Fisker already had major Silicon Valley backing. The lead investor was Ray Lane and John Doerr, legendary venture capitalists at Kleiner, Perkins, Caufied & Byers. A company called Tesla was looking like Fisker's chief competition. But the Fisker model appealed to me on a couple of fronts. First, it was an electric car that would allow you to go 150 miles on a charge but that also had a nine gallon gas tank, just in case. And, while Tesla was going the non-dealer route, Fisker would work within the automobile establishment, using existing, high-end BMW dealerships as its dealers.

Plus, Google the first model—Karma—and take a look for yourself: It was a way cooler designed car than anything Musk had come up with.

We ultimately invested in Fisker. At first, things were great. Karma was being built overseas—it would take a while to move operations to Delaware—and Fisker had cars on the road and glowing reviews and celebrities like Justin Bieber and Leonardo DiCaprio driving them too. We brought a bunch of the cars in from Delaware for an event we had at Xfinity Live! near the Philly sports stadiums. Our attendees got to drive the Karma on the surrounding streets and sign up to buy them. Grown adult men were giddy about this socially conscious new plaything.

Fisker came oh, so close to making it. But a couple of things happened to seal its fate. First, they lost more than three hundred cars during Hurricane Sandy, a $32 million loss. Second, the entire clean-tech industry became a political football that was kicked around during the 2012 Presidential election cycle.

But this is the business of venture capital. We take our shots; if you don't take shots, you'll never make a basket. There will be times when you get your shot blocked, but that does not mean that you should not take another shot after that.

Towards the end of the Fisker run, we had an opportunity for one more Hail Mary investment. Even though things didn't look good, we invested a little more money. Why? Because there was a glimmer of hope and I didn't want to be that guy who sat on the sidelines in a comeback story. It reminded me of how, at the eleventh hour—and between Thanksgiving and Christmas, no less—we raised $77 million to ultimately jump-start the sale of Take Care to Walgreens.

But there was another reason. I wanted to support the team and the entrepreneur, and make sure we did everything we could to help this thing work. When times get tough and things look bleak, that's no time for venture capitalists to cut and run.

So, Fisker went bankrupt and we lost our money. But I'd do it all again in a heartbeat, because so much is simply the luck of the draw. If Sandy doesn't hit when it did, if Presidential candidate Mitt Romney doesn't call out Fisker by name...who knows?

Grudgingly I have to hand it to Musk: He has infused the latest and greatest technologies inside his cars. Friends of mine have Teslas, and it definitely pains me to see Tesla's on the road today. We were so damn close. This venture capital game? It's not for the faint of heart.

THE GOSPEL ACCORDING TO WAYNE KIMMEL

If you're doing something that is truly revolutionary, then you're doing something others can't fathom yet. You're inventing the future. If you're pursuing something new, people are going to think you're nuts—until, in retrospect, they conclude that you were a genius all along.

Don't Be Afraid
To Be The Genius

Julian Krinsky is one of those guys. Self-made. Passionate. Nonstop energy. Bold ideas. Indomitable will. He was a pro tennis player from South Africa who made it to Wimbledon and the French Open and then relocated to Philadelphia's Main Line with hardly any money in his pocket. He started teaching tennis, founded a tennis camp, and soon was on his way to building an empire of exclusive summer camps – Julian Krinsky Summer Camps, focusing on everything from architecture to business, in partnership with the Wharton School.

In 1999, as he was just starting to branch out from traditional sports camps, Julian asked if I'd kick off the guest speaking lineup at his Leadership in the Business World ("LBW") program. It is a five-week, very exclusive program for rising high school seniors. Getting into the program is a highly competitive affair and it makes great sense for the University of Pennsylvania's Wharton School: It's actually a great recruiting tool for admissions.

I've now kicked off LBW for about 15 years in a row, and it blows me away who is in the room. The highest of achievers, with SAT and grades that are off the charts. The children of top business executives like Comcast's Brian Roberts to American Express' Ken Chenault have been in the audience, paying rapt attention to me.

That first year, I centered my talk around—what else?—building relationships. I brought my Nike shoebox in, pointing to the business cards. "This is your Gold," I said. "Your contacts are your gold." You never know who will help you, or who you will help in the future. Or what business you might end up being in." I'd bring along my shoebox filled with candy, stand on a desk, and announce that I had a special surprise for them... and then I'd start throwing Blow Pops and Tootsie Pops to—and sometimes at—them. I wanted to make it fun and memorable, because my parents had sent me to a business camp in Delaware the summer before my ninth grade year and I was bored to tears. The only thing I remember from it was there was a really pretty Italian girl there. She wasn't exactly feeling the Kimmel vibe.

Every year, I preach the power of relationships to these kids, but I also urge them to apply that same wisdom amongst themselves. "Get each other's contact information," I say. "The most important thing you're getting out of these five weeks is that you're meeting one another. Connect with each other on Facebook, Instagram or LinkedIn and just stay in touch – you have a special LBW bond for life. Half of you will probably be back at Penn next year, but either way—you're all going to be really successful. Start collecting contacts now."

Once you are connected to someone on a social networking/social media site, you are basically connected with them for life. When they update information about themselves or post something on their page, you will be able know about it.

My favorite day in the world is the day that one of my contacts has a birthday Why? Because it gives me a great opportunity to check in with them and simply wish them a happy birthday. It shows your contact that you thought of them, but you never know what that could bring. Many times, I will also use their birthday as a way to take a look at their posts and see if there are ways that we can help one another.

What's crazy is there have been some amazing stories that have come out of those LBW camps. One day I was listening to the Wharton Small Business show on Sirius radio and a really cool startup was featured, and the founders were talking about how they'd first met and incubated their idea during Krinsky's camp.

Some of the Wharton folks get annoyed when I tell the kids that they should ask every speaker who comes in for their business card and they should follow up with an email, thanking them for their visit. I think the Wharton people were afraid that these kids would annoy the speakers. But I believe I was teaching them what they needed to do in order to be successful. Other LBW speakers include Michael Rubin, who sold GSI Commerce for $2.4 billion to Ebay and is now Executive Chairman of sports merchandiser Fanatics, David Schlessinger of Five Below (and, before that, Zany Brainy...and, before that, Encore Books). Being thanked doesn't annoy these guys! Don't write a long paragraph, I say. Just say who you are and that you enjoyed their talk. And close with something like: "Thank you so much for taking the time to come in and speak to us, I look forward to staying in touch with you in the future." And that's it — sign off. They will be your contacts for life.

My "top secret" tip that I give to groups I speak to is to say "please" and "thank you." I put up a slide on the screen with a photo of Barney, the children's character. Because it's all about "please" and "thank you." And then I get really practical: "You probably don't want to send a very busy CEO an email at 11 am on a Monday," I say. "It will not be noticed. But if you send it at 2 am on a Monday or at 6 am on a Thursday as he's walking into work, you might just get a 'thank you' in response. Boom— you're on his radar!"

Once, I was about to deliver my LBW speech at Penn, when I detected a buzz in the room. Turns out, the Woz was in the house. The Woz! Steve Wozniak, the guy who built the Apple Computer, along with Steve Jobs. He was on campus for something totally unrelated. So I called an audible and started my speech off with:

"So what are you all doing here listening to me?" I said. "If I were you and I had an opportunity to meet Steve Wozniak, I would leave this room right now and go find him."

I could see the panic-stricken look in the eyes of the folks from Wharton. They didn't want the room to empty out. So, instead, I turned it into a discussion about how to approach the Woz, what to say. And I urged them to find him after our event. A few hours later, I got an email from a bunch of these high school kids, and this is why they're so much smarter than me. They not only went searching for him, they found him. And they not only talked to him, they made themselves memorable to him. "We got him to autograph our Macs," they told me. How cool is that? That's a better autograph than any athlete's—because he autographed the actual product. Tom Brady can't autograph a touchdown pass! Those kids created a memory for themselves that will stay with them forever. It made me feel great. And I'm sure Wozniak loved it.

Gradually, I started accepting more and more speaking gigs. In recent years, speaking engagements have taken up much of my time. Nowadays, it seems like every day there's another opportunity to be on a panel in front of young entrepreneurs, aspiring and otherwise. In fact, I've resolved to try and never refuse an invitation to speak to a group. Why? I wish that there would have been these types of discussions and public forums back when I was first coming out of college. I went by gut, freezing my butt off outside that Radnor Hotel, trying to get my cards into enough hands. I wish I'd had the chance back then to listen to someone who had been where I was.

But it's also because I feel like I owe it to the entrepreneurial community. I tell aspiring entrepreneurs that it's okay to feel crazy or have crazy ideas. You should be crazy. Remember that first Think Different commercial from Apple when Steve Jobs came back to Apple as CEO—"Here's to the crazy ones." I always play that ad when I speak. "If you have an idea and your mom and dad think you're crazy or your boyfriend thinks you're crazy," I say, "you just may be on the right path. Because you may be seeing things other people can't see. That's what Steve Jobs was talking about."

I feel like my job is to unlock the entrepreneurial spirit that I'm convinced is somewhere inside everyone. Everyone can be an entrepreneur. It just takes the courage to be different. "It's scary to think of yourself telling everyone, 'You know that thing you're doing? In five years, no one will be doing it anymore, you'll be doing *my* thing.'" I say. "That's scary. Because people may ostracize you. They may think you're one of the crazies. They'll look at you funny. They'll wonder who the hell you think you are. But you may be the genius. Don't be afraid to be the genius." It's only in retrospect, after all, that genius seems predetermined and inevitable.

See, college was great. I broadcasted the University of Maryland basketball and football games. Rubbed elbows and ate Maryland crab soup in the press box with ESPN's "Pardon the Interuption" guys (Tony Kornheiser and Michael Wilbon) when they were merely reporters at The Washington Post. I had a great social life and got good grades. But no professor ever said to me, "Follow your dreams. Think big. Chase your passions. Go for it." All I knew was I was going to follow in Dad's footsteps like every nice Jewish boy and become a lawyer. I didn't know much about the business school and I certainly did not know what an entrepreneur was.

So I floated along. Luckily, later, when he saw how much it meant to me, my Dad told me to go pursue my vague business dream instead of continuing to groom me to take over his law firm. Just by saying that, he allowed me to take a deep breath and just run. I had no idea what I was running toward, but I felt like I had some wind at my back because he told me it was okay. I was running free, with Kimby at my side, being my amazingly supportive wife. I had confidence. So now I try to do the same with every young person I come across and with the CEOs of my companies. I wish someone had done the same for me when I was in college.

Of course, these last ten years, everyone wants to be the next Zuckerberg. This is the Shark Tank generation, now that Mark Cuban's show is all the rage. Being a college age entre-preneur is seen as cool. But I tell kids all the time the goal of college is not to find your cofounder. "You're here to make friends, develop relationships, and be open to see where they lead," I say. But mostly, I tell them not to deny themselves the joys of the moment. "You're here to have sex. You're here to break up. You're here to make up. You're here to learn. Try dif-ferent things. Experiment. Have fun."

Notice I didn't say "you're here to fail." I hate the whole "fail fast" movement, this school of thought that it's okay to fail because that's where the lessons are. Failing is never a good thing. You should experiment, yes, and if things don't work out, shrug it off. Sometimes things just don't work out. It's okay. But we shouldn't glorify failure, as if it were an integral part of a successful plan. That failing conversation is one of my pet peeves.

One of the reasons I enjoy speaking with diverse groups about entrepreneurship, networking and giving back is that I learn from every group. I'm obsessed with consumer-facing products, so every group I speak to is a kind of focus group. I want to learn about their habits—what they buy, how they communicate—so I can better understand the possibilities for my companies. I ask questions all the time, trying to discern consumer trends. A few years ago, for example, it seemed like using email to connect with people was on its way out. Texting was where how you wanted to reach people, because you can only reach them if you're where they are. But now email seems to be making a comeback, at least in my anecdotal experience.

Plus, even when I'm talking to high school kids, don't think I'm not networking. I tell kids all the time, "I may be working for you in ten years." They look at me in disbelief, as though they expect me to know what I'm going to be doing for the rest of my life. But part of the fun is that I don't know. A few years back, I was part of a group that tried to buy the NBA's Philadelphia 76ers. I still want to own a pro sports team some day. You never know what opportunity lies ahead if you are in the game.

I tell young entrepreneurs that I'm advising, "Hey, who knows? You may become the CEO of Nike. Maybe I'll come work for you." Or maybe someone I've mentored will one day want to have a venture capital division of her multi-billion dollar company—and I'll go run it for her. I've had this talk with thousands of young people by now, and it's pretty cool. We stay in touch. I see when they graduate college. When they get their first job. Get married. Take a company public. I'm in the business of building lifelong relationships, and you never know where they're going to lead.

When I address a tech group, I'm keenly aware of the possibility that any one of these people staring back at me from the audience could very well one day be the CEO of a company I invest in. And I tell them that. "Listen, if you think you have a groundbreaking idea, reach out to me, I want to hear it," I say. "I may not know anything about the industry you're planning on disrupting, and I don't get involved with things I don't know about because I want to make sure I can add value. But who knows? Who knows where a conversation will lead until you have it?" Furthermore, I am always on the hunt for top talent for my portfolio companies.

So, yes, when I spend all this time spreading the Gospel According to Wayne, I'm giving back to the entrepreneurial community. And it's a blast to help people. But I'm also saying, "Hey, let's see if we can do business together." It's not all altruism. You can do good and also benefit from your good works at the same time.

Some of the best people I have met have come to my attention because of the speeches I give. Remember, that's how Tony Bifano and I first hooked up back in the day—coming up to me after my talk was this wild-eyed, fast-talking visionary. A few years back, speaking at the University of Maryland, my alma mater, a young man by the name of Danny Harvith sought me out. Danny interned for me and then I ended up hiring him; today, he's a leader of Philly's vibrant tech scene.

In my talks, I tell people not to send me an impersonal message inquiring about our internship program or if we're hiring. "Tell me you heard me speak at such-and-such," I say. "That will remind me—we shared a moment. If we spoke, tell me, 'I was the kid wearing the yellow sweater.' Self-identify yourself so you stand out!"

That's why I tell everyone—and I mean everyone—that they should be on social media all day, everyday. Back when I was starting out, I had to hustle like crazy to get my name in the Philadelphia Inquirer or the Philadelphia Business Journal. But now you can be your own publisher. And you should have your own personal website, too. Because that tells the story of you and you want people who Google you to find out from you what you're all about. You can be in control of the message of your own brand.

And, for someone like me, when you watch those brands grow and take off? That's the coolest thing. Take Daniel Fine, for example. I knew Daniel when he was a little kid through his parents. His Dad is the Chairman of Anesthesiology at Einstein Healthcare Network, where I sit on the Board of Trustees and his Mom ran major brands like Modell's Sporting Goods, iVillage, Victoria's Secret PINK, and Glamour Magazine. He was in

If you are building a company and people think you are doing something crazy, you are probably moving in the right direction.

the audience at one of those early LBW presentations. He went to Wharton and started setting the world on fire building businesses. Before he even graduated, he was featured in the New York Times for having started four successful companies—yes, four. They included his company, Glass-U, a maker of foldable sunglasses bearing the licensed brands of universities.

While Daniel was a student at the University of Pennsylvania, I told him I wouldn't be involved in his businesses because I wanted him to graduate. I knew his parents wanted him to get a degree and I didn't want to see him short-circuit his education. Students can get blinded by the tech star dropout story. Look, if you really believe you're that kind of rarity, go for it. But I don't think you can be a fulltime student and a fulltime entrepreneur. Because if you have to miss a meeting to take a chemistry test, that's not being an entrepreneur. Being an entrepreneur is 24/7 and being a college student is 24/7. Because it's not just about going to class, it's also about immersing yourself in a campus culture. It's about meeting people and developing relationships and experiencing the ups and down of being between the ages of 18 and 22. What's the rush?

I wanted to see Daniel wait to start his business after graduation, but what makes him unstoppable is—of course— he went ahead anyway. But at least he stuck it out and graduated. And now that he is a college graduate, I've helped him raise capital and build relationships. I'm on his Board and even made some calls to Penn administrators to help get his company its first office.

Why help people in this way? I think when most people give back, it's rarely totally selfless. When you're generous with your time or your money, it's because doing so makes you feel good. It's good in and of itself to give back, but if something good can come out of it for you, too—all the better. I tell aspiring entrepreneurs all the time that it's okay to be selfish—if it's for a good cause. I spend time mentoring young people because it makes me feel good, and because my business has benefitted mightily from these relationships over the years.

That's also why I'm so heavily involved with countless nonprofits. In the late Nineties, I went to an event at the Locust Club, a private club primarily for the Jewish business community in Philadelphia, that has since closed. I didn't even know such a place existed. That's when I first heard about the Jewish Federation of Greater Philadelphia. We weren't observant when I was growing up; I was Bar Mitzvah'd, but we weren't religious. The only thing my Dad would say about being Jewish was that "Jews are tough, and Kimmels are tough." Now, Kimby and I are not super religious either, but we do typically light Shabbat candles, bless our children on Friday nights and are involved in the Jewish community in the Philadelphia region.

So at the Locust Club I learned about all these Boards and charities. And the people on those Boards were the people I wanted to emulate. They were the ones that live in the rarified air; nonprofit boards were loaded with Philadelphia's movers and shakers.

So I just started going to charity events. Sometimes it cost me a lot of money. Then I started to observe that there never really seemed to be a guest list, so I just started dressing the part and walking right in. I would attend multiple events each night. And I'd be rubbing elbows with the people who ran the city.

I started to see David L. Cohen, the one-time Chief of Staff to Mayor Ed Rendell who went on to become Comcast's Executive Vice President, at almost every event I went to. I sometimes would read in the newspaper about an event that he was at and I would get upset if I'd missed it. So, I started stalking Cohen. I'd go to the Pennsylvania Society parties in New York that I knew he'd be at just to have passing conversations with him. When Comcast owned the NBA's Philadelphia 76ers, I remember going to games and seeing him in the stands, a brown legal folder and stack of papers stretched out on his lap. He was working while watching his team in his arena! I wanted that. (Years later, when I was part of that group that tried to buy the Sixers, I'm sure a part of me was planning on reenacting that scene if the deal had gone through).

As time went on, I served on the Einstein Healthcare Network Board of Trustees, the Board of the Kimmel Center for the Performing Arts, Jewish Relief Agency, and Jewish Federation of Greater Philadelphia. Through these organizations, you start to understand just how much of a positive difference you can make in people's lives. And, on a practical level, the contacts you make in the nonprofit world positively impact your own business life. I felt like I was getting an MBA just from listening to and learning from the CEO's of these organizations and from other Trustees.

At Jewish Federation, I became the Treasurer and chair of the Finance and Compensation committees. You meet a lot of financial types including money managers and bankers in that role, great contacts to have when you're raising capital. Ultimately, I was asked to serve on the Board of the Jewish Federation of North America, which has allowed me to meet the most successful Jewish philanthropists and business people in the world, some of whom I've invested with.

Don't get me wrong, getting involved in charitable causes for me doesn't come with any quid pro quos. It's more about inviting good karma. I don't walk around with my hand out. Instead, I try to serve others, work hard to make the world a better place and fully believe that if you help others, good fortune starts to come back around to you.

I got that message about serving and helping others at home when I was 17. This book is meant as a blueprint for professional success; I never wanted it to be the "Wayne Kimmel Story." But there was something in my private life that shaped who I am to the very core, and I can't help but think it similarly influenced all of the business philosophies you've been reading about.

My brother was once my cousin. Larry Kimmel was once Larry Spiller, and he was my first cousin. On December 31, 1987, Larry, his parents, Judy and Paul, and two brothers, Harvey and David, boarded a six-seat plane to fly to Vermont for a ski vacation. My uncle had a commercial pilot's license. The plane got caught in a wind shear 90 feet from the runway. Larry's parents died in the crash and his brothers were fatally wounded. For some reason—most likely the fact that he was in a seat with his back to the pilot—Larry was the only survivor.

I was 17 at the time. My sister Michelle was 14 and my sister Karen was 8. As a family, we decided that we now had a brother. It was Karen's idea to give up her bedroom for Larry. Longtime family friend Joe Biden spoke on the Senate floor about how my parents reacted to this terrible tragedy:

> "You hear a lot of talk these days about family values, but the Kimmels and Larry Spiller, that nine year old boy, have lived out what in reality is an old fashioned notion," the then-Senator said. "That families are there for one another. We have an expression in my family. After my wife and daughter were killed, I came home from the hospital, my two sons were in the hospital, and my sister had already moved into my house. She didn't ask anything...We have an expression in our family: If you have to ask, it's too late. Well, the Kimmels didn't have to ask; they just decided and they acted."

Morton and Marcia Kimmel didn't just act—they acted and, in the process, they modeled something for their kids. One of the first things they did was form a Foundation to aid other kids who have suffered similar loss, but who weren't quit as fortunate to have another loving family welcome them so openly.

At 17, I was playing varsity basketball and baseball and thinking about girls when my 9-year-old brother walked into my life. And I got the message loud and clear: There are other people in this world. Today, Larry Kimmel is my best friend and hero. And every time I do something for charity, I think of the huge commitment my parents made and I realize that serving on Boards and mentoring ambitious young people is the least I can do.

THE GOSPEL ACCORDING TO WAYNE KIMMEL

I feel like my job is to unlock the entrepreneurial spirit that I'm convinced is inside everyone. Everyone can be an entrepreneur. It just takes the courage to be different.

The Real Deal

In 2012, Hal Rosenbluth invited the investors of his latest ground breaking company, CareCam Health Systems, to his sprawling North Dakota ranch. CareCam is another technology company disrupting the healthcare system and has developed a comprehensive health management solution. It was a no-brainer investment for me, because it reimagines an industry in desperate need of reinvention and because it was the product of Hal's fertile brain — and, thanks to the wild success of Take Care Health Systems, I already had proof positive that he sees the future.

Anyway, Kimby and I went out to Hal's for some fun and good old-fashioned Western R&R. Hal likes to say that, if you really want to know who somebody is, spend time with him on the ranch. Now, I'm no Roy Rogers, but it was a point of personal pride when Hal once praised me for "Cowboying up real good."

On one of our first mornings at the ranch, I went for a run. I ran out to the two-mile mark, walked back to the 1 mile mark, and then ran back in. When I got back to the lodge next to Hal's ranch, Kimby was with Jon and Jill Powell. Jon was a personal investor in CareCam; for roughly the last quarter century, he'd run Kravco, a leading private real estate developer and property management company started by his father. His holdings included the iconic King of Prussia Mall — one of the largest in the world.

That's about all I knew about him, but I was about to find out a whole lot more. Turns out, that morning Jon was also just back from a run.

"It's beautiful out there, isn't it?" he said. "How about that view when you get to the highway?"

Um, what? "Isn't the highway at the 4 mile mark?" I asked.

"Yeah, I ran on the highway for a half-hour and then ran back," Jon said, totally matter-of-factly.

You know me, if I'm impressed by something, chances are it's not going to be an unexpressed thought. "You know how far that is?" I practically shrieked. "And you're back already?"

Jon is a shy guy about his accomplishments, whether in business or fitness. But I was instantly intrigued. It helped that Kimby and Jill really hit it off. We spent that whole trip together. I learned that Jon is an Ultraman.

"Is that like a triathlete?" I asked.

"Yeah, that's like a warmup," he said. The Ultraman World Championships competition consists of a 6.2 mile open ocean swim, a 261 mile cross-country bike ride and a 52 mile ultra-marathon run. I sat there, slack-jawed, asking question after question about the physical challenges Jon had taken on through the years. I heard all about the Furnace Creek 508 bike race, billed as the "Toughest 48 hours in Sport": 508 miles through Death Valley.

Jon's athleticism intrigued me from the start. In business and in life, I'm attracted to athletes. If you've been an athlete, you understand that business is a game. I remember my Dad telling me that, at the conclusion of a trial, win or lose, he'd approach opposing counsel, offering to shake hands. "You could always tell who the athletes were," he said, because those were the guys who would shake hands. They were passionate in the heat of battle, but sportsmanlike the moment the final whistle had blown. They understood that there's always a winner and a loser.

Also, business is competitive. When I speak publicly, I'm always using words like "hustle," "drive," and "resilience." Well, here was a guy who was basically able to trick his mind into believing that he could swim 6 miles, bike 260 miles and run a double marathon — all over three days. You've got to be driven. In business — particularly in startups, where everyone will tell you you're crazy— you've got to have that kind of resilience.

A friendship was born. Jon is a great guy, the life of the party, a no-nonsense businessman with a charitable streak. I learned many things from Ian Berg, but one of the best lessons was when he'd insist that, before making an investment, we have dinner with the CEO we were thinking about backing —and their spouse. "I want to see how they get along, how they treat each other, and how they treat the wait staff," Ian would say. It was always funny to me that this gruff, tough-as-nails character would care what kind of a marriage a CEO had. But he was right. Particularly in the startup world, you're talking about starting an intimate relationship together. It helps to examine the other intimate relationships in a prospective partner's life. Jon's relationship with Jill was just like mine with Kimby. I came to rely on Kimby's take on these matters, and she enjoyed our dinners with Jon and Jill as much as I did.

After our time together at Hal's ranch, I called him to get a sense of Jon Powell. "What's up with this guy, Jon?" I asked. "I really like him."

Hal, not given to effusively praise anyone or anything, simply said, "He's the real deal." That was enough for me. This guy and I were going to be tight.

Professionally, Jon and I first put our heads together on a project to bring a Microsoft Reactor innovation center to Philadelphia, the first of its kind after San Francisco. This could be a game-changer for our city and our motivation was fueled by a shared sense of civic responsibility.

Still, it was a surprise when Jon suggested we go beyond that one-off project and form a true partnership. Remember how my relationship with Ian was, to borrow a Yiddish phrase, "beschert"? Meant to be? So was this. The timing was right. Jon was looking to do something new and exciting, and new and exciting is what I do. And, while I was itching to start my next fund, I was thinking more and more about how the physical and digital spaces were colliding.

The smartest entrepreneurs I knew were bridging those two worlds. Michael Rubin, whose company Fanatics, the world's leading online seller of licensed sports merchandise, was suddenly operating brick and mortar stores. Same with Jeff Bezos and Amazon. My portfolio company, Indiegogo was embarking on partnerships with major retailers.

That's the future. The more I thought about it, the more convinced I was that, in the years to come, people will not just sit at home in their underwear all day, ordering food from Seamless or GrubHub, buying stuff on Amazon, crowdfunding their projects on Indiegogo, and using Skype for their meetings. I'd invested in a co-working space and I saw firsthand the degree to which people yearned to be out and about. As big as ecommerce is, it only makes up about 10 percent of retail sales today. And here was Jon Powell suggesting we team up, someone with relationships with every retailer in the world, from Neiman-Marcus to Foot Locker.

So we decided to start a venture capital fund together, which we're raising as I write this. As with my previous two funds, we'll look to support smart and nice entrepreneurs who are building game-changing companies. But we'll also look to help bridge the distance between the physical and digital worlds, because great opportunity lies in that space.

The goal of college is not to find your cofounder. You're there to develop relationships, and be open to where they lead. Don't deny yourself the joy of the moment. You're at college to have sex, break up, make up. Experiment. Have a great time!

Besides, Jon has risk-taking in his blood. His late father, Arthur Powell, and his business partner, borrowed $50,000 and eventually turned their company, Kravco, into one of the largest private shopping mall and management companies in the country. But, as is so often the case, Kravco's success was only inevitable in hindsight. When Jon's father built his first shopping mall in the early '60s, the conventional wisdom was that he was crazy. Who is going to go inside to shop? the naysayers asked. And why would the stores agree to the concept, seeing as how they'll just be competing against one another?

Well, look what happened. The concept of "the mall" became iconic, and retail stores were eager to get into them because that's where the customers were.

The skepticism Jon's father encountered feels familiar. Everything I've invested in has seemed crazy at the time. Think of it: Who needs to order food online? You're going to see a nurse practitioner at the drug store — are you kidding me? Crowdfunding? Crowd what?

And now Arthur Powell's son and I will be proving the doubters wrong with a venture capital fund that fills out the space between the physical and digital —a logical next step for consumer-facing companies. In that sense, our fund will be a way to honor Jon's Dad and his vision.

Jon often talks about how he "hit the jackpot" when referring to his relationship with his Dad. Our relationships with our Dads has bonded us. "You know, you talk a lot about your Dad," Jon once said to me. "I'd like to meet him." So we had a dinner with my Dad, along with Jon's brother Dick and my brother Larry, followed by taking in a college basketball game between the University of Delaware and Villanova, the eventual 2016 NCAA Champion. It was a great night, with lots of laughs and stories.

We're working hard on fundraising, but we're also intrigued by another development and opportunity that had Jon looking at me on a San Francisco street in mid-January and saying, "I think we're witnessing history in the making."

He was talking about what President Obama referred to as our "Cancer Moonshot" in January 2016 during his last State of the Union address, when he put Vice President Biden in charge of, as he put it, "a new national effort" to cure cancer.

We were there for the J.P. Morgan Health Care Conference and the StartUp Health Festival. Howard Krein, Chief Medical Officer of StartUp Health, is part of the Biden-led Moonshot effort.

The Moonshot is just getting underway, but what is already clear is that innovation and entrepreneurship will be critical to this final, heroic push to finally eradicate the scourge of cancer. It's a way for all of us to honor Beau Biden, who we loved, but even more than that, it's a way for us to put our skill sets to work for something bigger than our own needs.

Yes, these are some exciting times. A new fund. Bringing a Fortune 50 company to Philadelphia — The Microsoft Reactor. Helping, in whatever way we can to advance the Moonshot. Serving our portfolio companies. Keeping an eye out for the next game-changing company. Working with non-profits to make the world a better place. As always, success will depend on tapping into the skills and values that you've read about up till now: The importance of personal relationships; the karma that comes when you put other people first; hustle; resilience. It's going to be a crazy ride. I'm fastening my seat belt. But I wouldn't have it any other way.

Back when I was starting out, I had to hustle like crazy to get my name in The Philadelphia Inquirer or the Philadelphia Business Journal. But now you can be your own publisher. You should have your own website. Because that tells the story of you and you want people who Google you to find out from you what you're all about. You can be in control of the message of your own brand.

A venture capitalist was born on April 30, 1970 to Morton and Marcia Kimmel in Wilmington, DE.

Tatnall School, 1987. To this day, lessons learned from sports informs my business.

We grew up with the Biden's in Delaware. Here, then-Senator Joe with Kimby and me at our house for a 2007 fundraiser during his presidential run.

At Maryland, I was going to be the next Howard Cosell, broadcasting here with my frat brother Marc Quint in 1989 at Cole Field House.

The Kimmel Team, L to R: Sabrina, dog Madison, Kimby and Hunter in 2013 at Sabrina's Bat Mitzvah.

Thirty

U N D E R

30

Stories by **Claire Furia Smith** Profiles by **Jill P. Capuzzo** Photos by **Brad Bower**

L ast February, we asked our readers to nominate their peers for selection into *PhillyTech's* first 30 under 30 issue. Then we sifted through the stack of applications for the best of the best.

Selecting 30 people in the high-tech industry who represent the brightest and most exciting to watch in the Philadelphia area is no simple task. We had to raise the bar for entry into this elite group, especially when you only look at a select population of people age 30 and under.

This region has produced some individuals who made national headlines, technology types who produce great innovations and people who

work behind the scenes to ensure that Philadelphia's voice is heard as a technology center.

While selection was difficult, the achievements of these 30 individuals made the process easier. These people may be moving too fast for even themselves to see how much they've attained in their short careers, and their accomplishments may be common knowledge in their circle of peers. Now the region will learn of their success.

We slowed these 30 exceptional people down long enough to share a glimpse into their lives.

SUSAN STAPLETON
EDITOR

24 : http://www.philly-mag.com

Wayne Kimmel
Eastern Technology Fund

I arrived! A local magazine highlights me as one of the regions tech leaders.

L to R, with the StartUp Health braintrust: Howard Krein, Chairman Jerry Levin and Steven Krein.

Speaking at a 2014 Israel solidarity rally. I tell students all the time to find a cause they're passionate about and stand up for it.

Celebrating the sale of Take Care Health Systems to Walgreens with Hal Rosenbluth, L, and Peter Miller, R, at Hal's North Dakota ranch. Cowboy up!

WHISTLE SPORTS
HALL OF FAME
NEWFRONT 2016

Portfolio company Whistle Sports pays tongue-in-cheek homage!

My business partner, Jon Powell, left, with former AOL CEO and Chairman Steve Case, right, during Case's 2015 Rise of the Rest Tour.

Kimby and me with our parents: L to R, Morton and Marcia Kimmel, Nancy and James Schwartzman.

Visiting my portfolio company Dwolla in San Francisco with, L to R, right-hand man Chad Stender, Dwolla COO Charise Flynn and Jon Powell.

Kimby and me at the opening of Einstein Hospital in Montgomery County, on whose Board I sit.

L to R, Larry Kimmel, Karen Kimmel Legum, Michelle Kimmel Penner

2015 Philly Venture Capital and Tech Community dinner at our house that we hosted.

The SeamlessWeb sticker on the door of a Wall Street restaurant. It was always my goal to have SeamlessWeb stickers right there with Amex, Visa and Mastercard stickers.

L to R, CEO of Lindi Skin Lindy Snider, University of Maryland President Wallace Low and Ike Richman of the Comcast Spectacor before a Villanova v. Maryland basketball game in Philadelphia. Go Terps!

Discussing innovation in healthcare on the SiriusXM Wharton Business radio show, January, 2016.

Wayne Kimmel is an entrepreneur, venture capitalist, philanthropist, tireless networker, and the author of *Six Degrees of Wayne Kimmel.*

He is the Managing Partner of SeventySix Capital, the venture capital firm he founded in 1999, and has invested in over 40 startup technology and healthcare companies, including SeamlessWeb (now GrubHub), Take Care Health Systems and NutriSystem.

Philadelphia Magazine named Wayne a Top Innovator. He is on the Boards of Jewish Federations of North America, Jewish Federation of Greater Philadelphia, Einstein Healthcare Network, and the Kimmel Center for the Performing Arts.

Among the Fortune 500 companies that have acquired his portfolio companies are Aramark, Intel, IBM, Walgreens and Yahoo!

His current top portfolio companies include Adwerx, Care-Cam Health Systems, Dwolla, Indiegogo, Lindi Skin, ReverbNation, StartUp Health, Thrive Commerce and Whistle Sports.

In addition, Wayne serves on the National Advisory Council of the Delaware Law School and was on the Advisory Board of the Robert H. Smith School of Business at the University of Maryland.

Wayne is a graduate of the University of Maryland at College Park and the Delaware Law School. He is passionate about Philly's pro sports teams, and, through his nonprofit work, making the world a better place. He lives in the suburbs of Philadelphia with his wife and their 2 children.